THREE TEACHERS OF ALEXANDRIA:

THEOGNOSTUS, PIERIUS AND PETER

THREE TEACHERS OF ALEXANDRIA:

THEOGNOSTUS, PIERIUS AND PETER

A STUDY IN THE EARLY HISTORY OF ORIGENISM AND ANTI-ORIGENISM

by

L. B. RADFORD, M.A.

Rector of Holt (dio. Norwich), sometime Fellow of
St John's College, Cambridge

CAMBRIDGE:
at the University Press
1908

CAMBRIDGE
UNIVERSITY PRESS

University Printing House, Cambridge CB2 8BS, United Kingdom

Cambridge University Press is part of the University of Cambridge.

It furthers the University's mission by disseminating knowledge in the pursuit of
education, learning and research at the highest international levels of excellence.

www.cambridge.org
Information on this title: www.cambridge.org/9781107445772

First published 1908
First paperback edition 2014

A catalogue record for this publication is available from the British Library

ISBN 978-1-107-44577-2 Paperback

VXORI DILECTISSIMAE
CONSORTI VITAE STVDIORVM AVCTORI
HOC OPVSCVLVM
DEDICATVR

PREFACE

M. DENIS, the brilliant French scholar who in 1884 gave to the world an elaborate study of the philosophy of Origen[1], dealt at considerable length with the great writers of the fourth and succeeding centuries who took a prominent part in the criticism or defence of the peculiar teaching of the famous scholar of Alexandria. But he was disappointingly brief in his treatment of the Alexandrian teachers who came between Origen and Athanasius. Yet they have an interest of their own. The half-century which they occupy includes the first high-water mark and the first ebb of the tide of Origenism. Its claim upon our attention has been obscured by the supreme importance of the great Arian controversy which absorbed the next generation. Dionysius, the scholar, the pastor, the converter of heretics, the healer of schism, has at length received

[1] J. Denis, *Philosophie d'Origène* (Paris, 1884).

the recognition due to a great bishop of Alexandria whose manifold services to the Church of his day far outweigh the theological indiscretion which incurred the criticism of his namesake of Rome[1]. But the minor Alexandrians who followed him in school and diocese remain yet unrepresented in English theological literature. It is the aim of this dissertation to do something towards the filling of this gap. Our knowledge of the three writers here selected for study,—Theognostus, Pierius, and Peter the Martyr,—depends partly upon the comments of Photius, the scholar-patriarch of Constantinople in the ninth century, but mainly upon fragments of their writings long accessible in the pages of Routh's *Reliquiae Sacrae* and Pitra's *Analecta Sacra* and Migne's *Patrologia*, and recently enriched by the discoveries and discussions of De Boor, Diekamp and Harnack. The present dissertation is an attempt to estimate the teaching of these three Alexandrians with special reference to their adherence or their opposition to the teaching of their great predecessor Origen.

M. Denis remarks that while Origen's exegesis passed in a chastened form into the work of the great fathers of the fourth century, his philosophy ran a far less favoured course. Their task was to define certain

[1] Feltoe, *Dionysius of Alexandria* (Camb. Patristic Texts, 1904).

doctrines forced to the point of definition by the needs
of their day. The splendid but dangerous task which
Origen had set himself was to push the frontier of
Christian speculation to the furthest legitimate point,
while yet keeping in such close touch with his base of
operations, the tradition of the Church's faith, that
some of the ground which he traversed might become
a permanent acquisition to Christian theology. But
his philosophy, to quote M. Denis, "was on too many
points antagonistic to tradition, too free and too
venturesome ever to become a theology." It might
have disappeared as a system to survive as a spirit
under different doctrinal forms. "But it can be
affirmed without fear of contradiction that Origen
had no successor even in the bosom of the school of
Alexandria. The teaching of Heraclas is unknown.
Dionysius seems to have done little but repeat Origen's
teaching, doubtless in a weakened and reduced form ;
nothing is known of that of Pierius ; that of Theognostus would be more important to know, if it is true,
as Athanasius says, that he did not content himself
with explaining dogma but like Origen raised and
discussed a number of questions by way of exercise
(ὡς γυμνάζων). From his time it seems that the school
stood on the defensive. If that is only probable of

Peter the Martyr, it is certain of Didymus, who explained, softened, mitigated, i.e. effaced in large part, the doctrines of the *De Principiis,* especially those on the dogma of the Trinity, on which he was completely orthodox, if we may believe Jerome. As for the last master who is mentioned, Rhodon, his name is all that is known[1]." It will be seen in the course of this dissertation that M. Denis underestimated the extent of our knowledge of Theognostus and Pierius; that what was known of their work then and what has since been recovered goes far to prove that in ability they were not unworthy successors, and in teaching were close disciples of Origen; and that in Peter the Martyr, during his episcopate, if not already during his tenure of the catechist's chair, the Church of Alexandria found a theologian who was not an Origenist on his defence but a vigorous opponent of all that was peculiarly Origenistic.

---

[1] Denis, *op. cit.* pp. 416, 417.

L. B. R.

31 *March* 1908

CONTENTS.

THEOGNOSTUS.

PRACTICALLY nothing is known of the life of
Theognostus. Eusebius and Jerome never mention his
name in their accounts of early Christian writers and
teachers. Philippus Sidetes[1] notes that he was head of

[1] The fragment of Philippus preserved by an unknown compilator
(Cod. Bodl. Barocc. 142, fol. 216) and edited in 1689 by Dodwell
(*Dissert. in Iren.* App. pp. 488–514) states the succession of catechists
as follows : Dionysius, Pierius, Theognostus, Serapion, Peter. Dionysius became catechist in 231–2 when Heraclas, the successor of
Origen in that office, became bishop of Alexandria. In 247–8
Dionysius succeeded Heraclas as bishop. By way of reducing the
remarkably long interval between this date and the activity of
Pierius in 309, if not later, Dodwell supposed that Dionysius retained
the office of catechist during his episcopate (247–264). It is an
unproven supposition. In any case the bishop would not be likely to
retain the office for more than a short time, perhaps until a suitable
successor could be found. Probably Philippus was wrong in his
chronology here as elsewhere (e.g. in making Pantaenus the disciple
and successor of Clement), and misplaced Pierius. Theognostus was
probably the earlier of the two. Athanasius mentions Origen and
Theognostus together as παλαιοὶ ἄνδρες (*Ep.* 4 *ad Serap.* c. xi.).
Eusebius places the presbyterate of Pierius under the episcopate of
Theonas, 281–2—300. Achillas, a fellow-presbyter of Pierius, afterwards an Arian, is described by Eusebius as τῆς ἱερᾶς πίστεως τὸ

the catechetical school. Stephanus Gobar (so we learn from Photius, *Cod.* 28) was surprised to find Athanasius referring to him and to Origen in terms of commendation. George of Corcyra in the twelfth century mentions him in a curiously unchronological list of Church teachers, —"Dionysius of Alexandria, Methodius, Clement of Alexandria, Pierius, Pamphilus, Theognostus, Irenaeus, and Hippolytus,"—all of whom George describes as having been led astray from the truth by human infirmity. "Certain of their sayings we cannot accept, though in other respects they have our highest admiration[1]."

It is as a writer that Theognostus is best known. Four fragments of his writings have survived. Athanasius in his fourth epistle to Serapion (c. xi.) quotes a passage on the sin against the Holy Ghost, and in his epistle on the definitions of the Nicene Council (c. xxv.)

διδασκαλεῖον ἐγκεχειρισμένος. The expression may be quite general, but it may refer to the catechetical office, in which case Achillas was either a colleague or assistant of Pierius (as Clement was of Pantaenus, and Heraclas of Origen for a time), or less probably his successor. Of Serapion nothing is known for certain. The whole succession should perhaps be stated thus : Pantaenus (180–200), Clement (200–203), Origen (203–231), Heraclas (231–2), Dionysius (231–2—247–8), Theognostus (247–8—282), Pierius (282– ?), Serapion, Peter (? –300). But the records are so scanty that we cannot be sure that this list from Theognostus to Peter is complete. See Bardenhewer, *Gesch. d. altkirchl. Litt.* ii. 168, 195, 199, 203; Harnack, *Altchr. Litt.* II. (*Chron.*) ii. 67, n. 4, and 71 ; Diekamp, *Theolog. Quartalschr.* 1902, p. 491.

[1] Quoted by Harnack, *Altchr. Litt.* I. 476.

a passage on the relation of the *ousia* of the Son to that
of the Father. Gregory of Nyssa (*Contra Eunom.* III. iii.)
ranks Theognostus along with the Arian Eunomius on
the ground that he describes the Son as an instrument
in the work of creation. Diekamp[1] has lately printed
and annotated a new fragment from an unknown
compiler, which deals with the scriptural terms applied
to the Son (λόγος, σοφία, εἰκών, ἀπαύγασμα and
κάτοπτρον), and dwells upon the fulness of the Godhead
in the Son and upon His likeness to the Father in
unity and immutability.

Fortunately Photius (*Cod.* 106)[2] has preserved for
us an account of a great work of Theognostus which
consisted of seven books and bore the title τοῦ μακαρίου
Θεογνώστου 'Αλεξανδρέως καὶ ἐξηγητοῦ 'Υποτυπώσεις.
The term " exegete" marks doubtless the catechetical
office of Theognostus. The title 'Υποτυπώσεις should
probably be translated " outlines" rather than " sketches."
It denotes at once brevity and system. From the
account which Photius gives of the work it was
evidently a comprehensive view of Christian doctrine.
The following is a table of its contents framed from
the information given by Photius :

---

[1] *Theologische Quartalschrift*, 1902, lxxxiv. pp. 481–494. The
earlier fragments are printed and annotated by Routh in his *Reliquiae
Sacrae*, iii. 407–422, and all four by Harnack in *Texte u. Untersuch.*
xxiv. (N. F. ix.) 3, pp. 73–92.

[2] Routh, *R. S.* iii. 412–414.

The remarks of Photius are clearly not a complete
account of the contents of each book, but merely
comments on various points which seemed to deserve
praise or blame. The style of the work, he says, was
simple and vigorous ; its diction had all the grace of the
Attic school without its affectation ; its sentences ran
easily ; and the claims of accuracy and clearness were
not allowed to impair the dignity of the subject.   In
the first book Theognostus set himself to prove that
God is the creator and to refute those who supposed
that matter is coeternal with God.   In the second he
argued " that the Father must have a Son" ; but in speak-
ing of the Son he described Him as a creature ($\kappa\tau\iota\sigma\mu\alpha$)
and as exercising authority only over rational beings,
and said other things too in derogation of the Son, like
Origen.   Photius tries to give Theognostus the benefit
of the doubt.   He may have been actually guilty of
" irreverence" (i.e. heterodoxy) like Origen ; or, to stretch
a point in his favour, he may have been stating an
argument rather than laying down a doctrine ; or again
he may have been accommodating himself to the lower

level of a hearer altogether unfamiliar with the Christian religion and unable to receive the whole system of the faith, and perhaps he held back part of the truth in the belief that any sort of knowledge of the Son was better for the hearer than absolute unfamiliarity and ignorance. Still, Photius proceeds, although such a hesitation to state the true faith might be neither unsuccessful nor unworthy as a method of oral discussion, it is a feeble defence to offer this excuse for the " irreverent" language of a written treatise intended for general circulation as a common standard of teaching. Similarly in the third book Theognostus stated the grounds for the belief in the personal existence ($\H{v}\pi\alpha\rho\xi\iota\nu$) of the Holy Spirit, but on other points was as wide of reason as Origen in his work *De Principiis.* In the fourth book he followed Origen in clothing spirits with attenuated bodies. In the fifth and sixth books he endeavoured to prove the possibility of the Incarnation, but much of the language of these books was absurd and reckless, especially his statement that the Son was limited in His presence on earth by time and space and only unlimited in His activity. In the seventh book, which (Photius says) bore the title "Of God's creative work," Theognostus was more orthodox in his teaching, and especially in what he said of the Son at the close of this section.

Upon these last remarks of Photius Diekamp built an ingenious theory with regard to the theological history

of Theognostus himself (*Theol. Quart.* 1902, pp. 489–491).
The seventh book unlike the others has a special title
(περὶ Θεοῦ δημιουργίας) which carries us back to topics
already discussed in book i.   It deals also with the Son,
and in this respect goes back also to the subjects of
book ii. and possibly books v. and vi.   The first six books
are a systematic sequence; the seventh is apparently a
supplementary section of the work.   Photius expressly
states that it was more orthodox, especially in its Christology.   Probably therefore it was a revision or correction
of earlier statements.   Diekamp ventures even to suggest
a possible occasion for this reconsideration.   Dionysius
of Alexandria in his controversy with the Sabellians of
the Pentapolis had made incautious use of the terms
ποίημα and γενητὸν with reference to the Logos, and in
reply to a letter from Dionysius of Rome had partly
indeed protested against misrepresentation of his earlier
language, but had also partly corrected or abandoned the
expressions that had given offence.   Perhaps Theognostus learned from his bishop's experience, and took
this opportunity to revise his view of the Logos and
His relation to the Father and to the world, and in
particular to explain or recall such a dangerous expression as the word κτίσμα.   Harnack however (*T. U.* pp.
79–82) gives good reason for doubting the premises
upon which this theory is built.   It is true that Photius
quotes the actual words of the title in the case of one
book only, viz. the seventh; but he mentions the sub-

jects of all the others but the second so distinctly that he seems to be recalling an actual heading of each book, and his reference to the contents of the second makes it quite clear that that book did deal with the Son, as we should expect from its place in the series. The supposition that the seventh book was a *retractatio* of topics already discussed is uncertain and unnecessary. The subject of creation indeed occurs in the first book and again in the seventh; but in the first Theognostus is dealing with the creative function of God and His relation to the material world, i.e. with the presuppositions of the Christian doctrine of creation, while the seventh apparently deals with the results of that creative action, i.e. with the world itself[1]. It is surprising perhaps to find this subject postponed to the end, but Harnack sees in this arrangement an illustration of the Alexandrian view which set the Incarnation in close connexion with the preexistence of the Son and in priority to the work of creation. We might add that this recalls the language of S. Paul, to whom the Incarnation was not only a historical fact but also the eternal purpose of God (e.g. *Eph.* iii. 11). As for the greater orthodoxy of this book, there was less room here for the peculiar views which would naturally come out

[1] Krüger (*Gesch. d. altchr. Litt.* 1893, p. 133) takes this book as dealing with the divine government of the world (*Gottes Weltregiment*), but surely δημιουργία is not οἰκονομία. Zahn (*Forsch. z. N. T. Kanon,* iii. 130) thinks it was a recapitulation of the whole theological system of the *Hypotyposeis.*

in the discussion of the Son, eternal or incarnate. The emphasis which Photius lays upon this orthodoxy need not be interpreted as implying a correction of earlier contents of the work; it is due rather to his desire to bring out the good points in Theognostus and in other ante-Nicene theologians as a set-off against the bad points which he cannot extenuate[1].

Harnack remarks that it is surprising to find no book in the *Hypotyposeis* dealing with man or with redemption or with Holy Scripture; but he suggests that the seventh book would naturally include the subject of man, and the fifth and sixth the subject of redemption. The subject of Scripture he thinks it was not necessary for Theognostus to discuss, as Origen had already devoted one of the books of his " First Principles" to that subject. But surely this reason would apply equally well to many other subjects in the " Outlines" of Theognostus, who would have been reduced to scanty materials indeed if he had abstained from anything more than gleaning or even from gleaning in fields already reaped. It would have been an instructive task to set the two works in detailed comparison; but the work of Theognostus has only survived in a few fragments and in a brief analysis by a late critic. As it is, we can only contrast the general plan of the two works. Origen divided his great work into four books. The first dealt with the nature of God, the

---

[1] Harnack, *op. cit.* p. 81.

Logos, the Holy Spirit, and the angels; the second
with the world and man, his restoration through the
Incarnate Word, and his destiny, eternal life; the third
with the freedom of the human will, the conflict between
good and evil, and the final triumph of good; the fourth
with the interpretation of Holy Scripture as the basis
of Christian doctrine. It is impossible to construct a
parallel in detail between the *De Principiis* and the
Hypotyposeis. We can only note that the first book of
the *De Principiis* contained the subjects which occupied
the first four books of the *Hypotyposeis*, viz. the Holy
Trinity and the angels, i.e. the invisible world of
spiritual beings. The second book contained the subjects which occupied the last three books of the work of
Theognostus, viz. creation and redemption, i.e. the visible
world and the destiny of man. Origen's last two themes,
freewill and revelation, i.e. the relation of man to God
and the relation of God to man, either lay outside the
scope of Theognostus or fell into a subordinate or
incidental position under the head of one or other of
the subjects for which he did find a distinct place.
It is just in those two great subjects that the difference between the work of Origen and that of
Theognostus lies. They are strictly questions rather
than subjects. The very title of Origen's work ($\pi\epsilon\rho\grave{\imath}$
$\dot{a}\rho\chi\hat{\omega}\nu$), denoting as it does not the elements of the universe but the first principles of a philosophy of religion,
describes the character as well as the contents of the
work. Origen is endeavouring to construct a science

of faith. The centre of Christian truth is the teaching
of Christ and His apostles, preserved and interpreted
by the Church, and received by the Christian in simple
faith which issues in holy living. But there is a circum-
ference as well as a centre, and it is within this circle
that knowledge (*gnosis*) finds its scope. It is the work
of Christian *gnosis* first "to trace the *how* and the
why of the simple *that* of apostolic teaching[1]," and
secondly to investigate those questions on which the tradition of the Church is silent or undecided. The basis
of this investigation is Holy Scripture in all its bearings,
historical, moral and spiritual, or in other words literal
and allegorical. This was the work of Origen. Theognostus on the other hand seems to have set himself
not to discuss principles of theology but rather to give
a systematic statement of Christian doctrine. His
material is subdivided more distinctly than Origen's;
and speculation seems to have found but slight space
in Theognostus in comparison with positive teaching,
though that teaching altogether was not free from ideas
that belonged to the speculative rather than to the
traditional side of Origenistic theology.

The aims of the two works were different; but that
the contents of the *Hypotyposeis* bore witness to the
Origenistic sympathies of their writer it is impossible to doubt in view of the comments of Photius.
Theognostus denied the eternity of matter; he

---

[1] Bardenhewer, *Gesch. d. altk. Litt.* ii. 135.

regarded the Son as a "creature" and confined His
operation to rational beings; he distinguished between
the teaching of the Son and the teaching of the Spirit;
he attributed a bodily existence to angels and demons;
and he limited the personal presence of the Son incarnate. In all these cases there is a parallel to the
teaching of Origen. We have now to examine in
detail the fragments which have survived from the
writings of Theognostus himself, and to estimate more
closely in the course of that examination the extent
of his dependence upon the great Christian thinker
whose work marked an epoch in the history of Greek
theology.

1. Photius observes that in the second book
Theognostus argued that the Father must have a Son;
but he gives no indication of the sort of arguments
(ἐπιχειρήματα) which Theognostus employed. It may
have been an inductive proof from statements of Holy
Scripture, or, more probably, a deductive proof from
the necessities involved in the idea of God. We are
reminded almost of the thought of Origen, that God,
being absolute goodness, must desire to reveal Himself
to man and can only reveal Himself through the Word.
Theognostus may have taken a similar line. It is
probable that the necessity of a divine Sonship is
regarded here in its manward aspect. To Origen the
Trinity is a Trinity required by and only recognised in
revelation and redemption. It was not until Augustine

that the Trinity in its internal relations was explained
by the necessity of love within the Godhead[1].

2. "In speaking of the Son he describes Him as a
creature," proceeds Photius (υἱὸν δὲ λέγων κτίσμα αὐτὸν
ἀποφαίνει). The actual use of the word κτίσμα is
doubtful. Photius may be quoting the exact word
used by Theognostus, but the language of Photius
(κτίσμα αὐτὸν ἀποφαίνει) looks rather as though he
were simply giving the gist of what he took Theognostus to mean. There is a similar doubt with regard
to Origen and Dionysius. Justinian in his famous
letter to the patriarch Mennas in 553 attributes the
offensive word to Origen, but it seems undiscoverable
in the extant writings of Origen[2]. Dionysius bishop
of Alexandria had about this very time used language
to the same effect, and Athanasius in defending the
orthodoxy of Dionysius speaks of the error in question
as the description of the Word as a ποίημα or κτίσμα
or γενητόν. But the word κτίσμα itself does not occur
either in the fragments of the letter which Dionysius
of Rome wrote against this error or in those of the
Alexandrian bishop's own *Apologia*. On the other
hand the Alexandrian bishop admits that he cannot
recall the precise wording of his first pastoral letter
which had raised the suspicion; he remembers using
the illustrations of the husbandman and the vine, the

[1] Bethune-Baker, *Intr. to Early Hist. of Chr. Doctrine*, p. 147.
[2] *Ib.*, p. 148, n. 2.

shipwright and the boat; and Dionysius of Rome turns to explain the text, κύριος ἔκτισέ με ἀρχὴν ὁδῶν αὐτοῦ (Prov. viii. 22), in a way which suggests that it had been used to justify such expressions as κτίσμα and ποίημα. If Theognostus could have replied to Photius, he would perhaps have defended himself very much as Dionysius had done. The bishop pointed out that he had used other illustrations,—the relation of a plant to its seed or root, and of a river to its source,—which ought to have corrected the misleading impression gathered from the more dubious illustrations, but that those truer illustrations had been ignored by his critics ; and he insisted that the words ποίημα and ποιεῖν were used in various senses, not merely in the sense of actual creation, both in profane and in sacred writers. The whole discussion is an eloquent lesson on the limitations and the dangers of human analogies used to explain divine relations[1]. We shall see presently that Theognostus had no idea of placing the Son in the category of created things, even if his use of the word Son is not proof enough in itself. But it is interesting to ask, what was the idea that led him to use the word κτίσμα or words to that effect ? Perhaps the answer is to be found in the question whether the Son had His origin in a necessity of the nature of God or in the free action of the will of God. This was a question which became

[1] Feltoe, *Dionysius*, pp. 165–176 ; Bethune-Baker, *op. cit.*, pp. 112–118.

urgent when the Arians insisted that such an act of
will must have preceded the coming of the Son into
existence, in which case He could not be eternal, and
told the orthodox triumphantly that the only alternative
was to admit the idea of compulsion. The question
had not yet been pushed so far in the third century;
but it may have been the fear of such a semblance of
compulsion that led Origen to speak of the Son as
"born of the Father, like an act of His will proceeding
from the mind[1]." The only necessity that Origen
recognised was the need of revelation, a need which
sprang from the goodness of God and from no outward
compulsion, and which found free expression in the will
of God. Was it this idea which lay behind the language
summed up in the word κτίσμα? It was a word which
misled or was misunderstood; but perhaps after all
what it was intended to convey was simply this, that
the being of the Son was the expression of the Father's
will as well as the outcome of the Father's nature.

3. The Arian sense of the word κτίσμα is ruled
out of consideration in this case by the appeal which
Athanasius makes as against the Arians to "the learned
Theognostus" (*Ep. de decret. Nic. Synod.* 25). The
language of the Nicene fathers, he says, was no new
thing; it was a reassertion of earlier teaching. "Learn

[1] *De Princ.* i. 2. 6. On this question of the generation of the Son
by will or of necessity, see Neander, *Ch. Hist.* (E. Tr. Bohn) ii. 310,
and Bethune-Baker, *op. cit.* pp. 194, 195.

then, ye Christ-hating Arians, that the learned Theognostus did not hesitate to use the phrase ἐκ τῆς οὐσίας, for that is what he says in writing about the Son in the second book of his *Hypotyposeis.*" Then follows the extract from Theognostus. "The *ousia* of the Son was not an invention from without nor an importation from things non-existent before. It was the offspring of the Father's *ousia,* as the radiance is of the light, as vapour is of water. The radiance is not the sun itself, nor is the vapour the water itself, nor again is it something foreign; and the *ousia* of the Son is not the Father Himself nor foreign to the Father, but an emanation from the *ousia* of the Father, the *ousia* of the Father undergoing no division thereby[1]; for as the sun remains the same and is not diminished by the rays poured forth by it, so the *ousia* of the Father underwent no change, the Son being its image[2]."

Harnack[3] thinks that Theognostus attributed to the Son a special *ousia* of His own, since he speaks not of

---

[1] οὐ μερισμὸν ὑπομεινάσης. Cp. Origen, *in Joh.* t. xx. § 16, against any μείωσις of the Father.

[2] οὐδὲ ἡ οὐσία τοῦ πατρὸς ἀλλοίωσιν ὑπέμεινεν, εἰκόνα ἑαυτῆς ἔχουσα τὸν υἱόν. Newman, *Arians of the fourth century,* p. 199, translates, "*though* the Son be its image," as if εἰκὼν implied a possibility of an ἀλλοίωσις in the original. But εἰκόνα is the emphatic word; an image is a representation of the whole of the original, not a separation of a portion of the original, and the reason why the *ousia* of the Father suffers no loss is simply that the Son's *ousia* is an *eikon* of the Father's.

[3] *Texte u. Unters.* xxiv. 3, p. 86 (1903).

"the Son" but of "the *ousia* of the Son." It is a doubtful inference. Theognostus would naturally speak of "the *ousia* of the Son" as he speaks of "the *ousia* of the Father." He is dealing throughout with the relation of the one to the other. But the question whether the one is different from the other must be determined by what he actually says about it, and the extract as a whole as well as the phrase ἐκ τῆς τοῦ πατρὸς οὐσίας is against the idea of such a difference as Harnack infers. It is rather in favour of Harnack's own earlier comment in his *History of Dogma* (ed. 1894, E. Tr. iii. 97), where he says that this passage "undoubtedly proves that Theognostus did full justice to the homo-ousian side of Origen's theology." The term "emanation" (ἀπόρροια) is used to express the origin of the one nature in the other, and then, as the idea of difference seems to be involved, is supplemented by the term "image" which contradicts that idea. The passage is a striking example of the need of care in the use of analogies. Radiance and vapour are illustrations which serve admirably to rule out the crude idea of the Son as a creation from an external source, and to define His nature as partaking of the essence of its source. The term "emanation," which covers the examples of radiance and vapour, connotes both the origin and the distinctness of that which emanates. But it involves also the idea of loss, if not of change, in the source of the emanation. The break-

down of the illustration at this point is tacitly confessed
by the substitution of a second illustration, viz. that of
an image. This new illustration conveys the idea of a
full and complete representation, and this idea is worked
out by Theognostus in another fragment (pp. 22 f.). But
it is used here because it has two advantages : (i) It
is free from the idea of change or loss affecting the
thing represented by the image. This idea of loss was
obvious in one of the two examples of emanation.
Evaporation means the draining of the source. Perhaps
this was the reason why Theognostus dropped the
analogy of vapour, and fell back on the analogy of
radiance, when he wanted to explain that the being of
the Son was in no sense a subtraction from the being
of the Father. The science of a later day with its
doctrine of the conservation of energy has robbed
Theognostus of this analogy also. But the illustration
of the sun undiminished by its shining still serves to
define the meaning of Theognostus. The Father's
ousia loses nothing of what it gives to the Son. (ii) At
the same time the term "image" corrects another defect
of the term "emanation." Vapour differs from water
in appearance. Perhaps that was a second reason why
Theognostus introduced the designation εἰκών, which
safeguarded the idea of the Son as a perfect revelation
of the Father.

To revert to the description of the Son as a
"creature," Harnack sums up his comments on this

extract with the judgment: "the indication of Photius
that Theognostus calls the Son a κτίσμα and sets Him
as Lord in relation to rational beings alone, is weightier
than this whole fragment[1]." It is not certain that
Theognostus actually used the unhappy word; but if
he did, its use must be counterbalanced by this fragment, not *vice versa*. The term κτίσμα must be read
in the light of the terms ἀπαύγασμα and ἀπόρροια.
Man may be called εἰκὼν as well as κατ᾽ εἰκόνα Θεοῦ,
but he is not called an ἀπαύγασμα or an ἀπόρροια of
God. Origen and Dionysius used ἀπαύγασμα to illus-
trate the eternity of the relation of the Son to the
Father. The light never existed without its radiance.
But an eternal κτίσμα is no "creature" in any sense of
the word as it is commonly understood.

4. It was the fault or rather the misfortune of the
Origenists that their language lent itself often to Arian
use. If Athanasius could appeal to Theognostus as a
witness to the phrase ἐκ τῆς οὐσίας, perhaps he could
appeal all the more pertinently because the Arians had
first appealed to Theognostus as an authority on their
side. Gregory of Nyssa remarks that the extreme
Arian Eunomius is not alone in describing the Son as
an instrument in the work of creation, for the like
error is to be found in the writings of Theognostus, who
says that "God, wishing to frame this world, first set
the Son before Him as a kind of standard of creation":

[1] *T. U.* p. 86.

c. *Eunom.* lib. iii. or. iii., τὸν θεὸν βουλόμενον τόδε τὸ πᾶν¹ κατασκευάσαι πρῶτον τὸν υἱὸν οἷόν τινα κανόνα τῆς δημιουργίας προϋποστήσασθαι. Gregory proceeds to argue that a thing which exists not for its own sake but for the sake of something else is of less value than the thing for which it exists. A plough is of less value than the life which it exists to feed. On the Eunomian theory of creation our Lord would be inferior in dignity to the world. Gregory is scarcely fair here even to Eunomius. He is certainly not fair to Theognostus. Origen himself had spoken of God as creating the world in accordance with ideas " previously brought to consciousness (προτρανωθέντας) in Wisdom," just as a house or ship is built after a plan in the builder's mind; but elsewhere he could say, " Christ is Creator as being the Beginning, inasmuch as He is Wisdom². " We lack a saying of Theognostus which shall similarly explain

¹ Harnack, *op. cit.* p. 87, takes τόδε τὸ πᾶν as meaning merely this world of ours, not the whole of the created universe, and remarks accordingly that Theognostus is in no way contradicting here Origen's idea of the eternity of creation. Origen denied the eternity of matter as a principle external to God (cp. Photius' description of Theognostus' first book as directed against the upholders of this eternity of matter, κατὰ τῶν ὑποτιθέντων συναίδιον ὕλην τῷ Θεῷ); but, regarding the creative function as necessarily eternal because it is a divine attribute, he was led to infer that it must have always been operative in creating a succession of worlds from nothing, e.g. *De Princ.* iii. 5; cp. Neander, ii. 281; Hagenbach, *Hist. of Christ. Doctrine* (E. Tr.), i. 187, n. 9.

² *In Joh.* i. 22; Bigg, *Christian Platonists of Alexandria*, p. 169, n. 1.

or redeem the words quoted by Gregory. But those
words are not themselves conclusively what Gregory
takes them to be. At first sight they do seem perhaps
to suggest the creation of the Son as the preparation
for the creation of the universe, and in that case they
may account for the attributing of the term κτίσμα to
Theognostus. But they are after all quite consistent
with the preexistence of the Son. Origen could speak
of Christ as the mind of God "containing in Himself
all the elements and forms of all creation[1]." Theognostus probably meant this and no more. The Son,
it should be noted, is the preexistent, not the incarnate
Son. Theognostus is not thinking of the Incarnation
being contemplated by the Father beforehand as His
model for the creation of humanity; he is thinking of
the eternal Son in Himself being contemplated by the
Father as the fulness of His own mind and the sum of
His own purpose for the whole world.

5. This idea of the Son as the expression of the
whole counsel of God is elaborated in the invaluable
fragment of the *Hypotyposeis* to which Diekamp gave
circulation in the *Theologische Quartalschrift* of 1902.
It is a discussion of the names or titles by which the
Son is described in Holy Scripture. The unknown
compiler who preserved the fragment prefixed to it the
warning note that in many other passages the writer
uses blasphemous language on the subject of the Son

[1] *De Princ.* i. 2. 2.

and of the Holy Ghost. This sounds like an echo of
Photius. The fragment may have owed its preservation
to its freedom from such " blasphemy," but Harnack is
scarcely justified in saying that it is therefore not to be
regarded as a representative specimen of the teaching
of Theognostus (*nicht als typisch angesehen, T. U.* xxiv.
3, p. 87). " The Scriptures," writes Theognostus, " give
the Son the names Word and Wisdom. He is called
the Word as issuing from the mind of the Father of the
universe[1], for it is plain that word is the noblest

[1] λόγον μὲν (ὀνομάζουσιν) οἷα δὴ <ἐκ τοῦ> νοῦ τοῦ πατρὸς τῶν ὅλων
ἐξιόντα. The words ἐκ τοῦ are a conjecture of Harnack's. Diekamp's
text is οἷα δὴ νοῦ κ.τ.λ. The precise construction is not easy to determine. (i) The order of the Greek will scarcely permit the rendering
" from the Father, the mind of the universe." This would be a
striking parallel to the language of Dionysius (Athan. *de sent. Dion.*
23) : ὁ πατήρ, ὁ μέγιστος καὶ καθόλου νοῦς. (ii) This parallel would
also hold if we could translate " from the mind, the Father of the
universe." Either rendering gives us the theology of the Alexandrian
school, which regarded the Father as the mind of the world, as
against the theology of the Apologists and Anti-gnostics, who described the Son as the mind (νοῦς) as well as the word (λόγος) and
the wisdom (φρόνησις) of the Father. See examples in Diekamp, *op.
cit.* p. 484. (iii) But the most natural rendering is " from the mind
of the Father of the universe." Diekamp is at great pains to prove
that this fragment leaves no room for any existence or conception
intermediate between the Father and the Son such as was recognised
by the Neo-platonists, who, according to Diekamp, distinguished three
entities, the ἕν (μόνας), the νοῦς, the λόγος. Diekamp is right in
laying stress upon the fact that Theognostus regards the Word as the
first and full expression of the Father's *ousia.* But he is strangely
incorrect, as Prof. Inge pointed out to me in a helpful criticism of
the original draft of this note, in his description of the Neo-platonist
trinity of being. That trinity consisted of the One (ἕν), the Mind

offspring of mind. But the Word is also an image
(εἰκών)¹, for the Word alone is entrusted with the outward conveyance of the thoughts that exist in the Mind.
Words however in us men (οἱ μὲν ἐν ἡμῖν λόγοι) are but
a partial enunciation of such things as are capable of
enunciation, and they leave some things unspoken,
treasured in the mind alone. But the living Word of
God² <interprets all the mind of God>. Wherefore
<the Word> is also called Wisdom, as that name is
better able to indicate the multitude of thoughts
(θεωρημάτων) contained in Him." Then follows a
passage in which the writer dwells upon the likeness

(νοῦς) and the Soul (ψυχὴ), as is evident from Plotinus (*Ennead.* v. i. 6
and 7; cp. Überweg's *Hist. of Phil.* i. 248, 249). Harnack, like
Diekamp, takes Πατήρ as = Νοῦς (*T. U.* p. 88), and notes in support
of this identification that Theognostus in this same fragment
identifies man and the mind of man, ἐν ἡμῖν being apparently parallel
to ἐν τῷ νῷ μόνῳ. This is too precise; ἐν ἡμῖν may merely mean " in
the case of us men." The mind is not distinct from man, but it is
not coextensive with man. Similarly " the mind of God " is not the
same thing as " God the mind." The language of Theognostus
seems to be intermediate between the Alexandrian identification of
Mind with the Father and the Neo-platonist separation of the
two. He rather regards the Mind as part of the Father's *ousia*.

¹ Diekamp cp. Origen *in Joh.* i. 42, τὰ τῆς ἀληθείας θεωρήματα οὐ
συνέχων ὁ πατὴρ ἐρεύγεται, καὶ ποιεῖ τὸν τύπον αὐτῶν ἐν τῷ λόγῳ, καὶ διὰ
τοῦτο εἰκόνι καλουμένῳ τοῦ ἀοράτου Θεοῦ.

² τὸν οὐσιώδη τοῦ Θεοῦ λόγον, i.e. having an *ousia* of His own, in
contrast to words that are only voice and sound; almost = " self-
existent," " personal " (usually ἐνυπόστατος). It is the emphatic
term of the sentence. The Word is the full interpreter *because* He is
οὐσιώδης, a speaking, not a spoken, word.

of the Son to the Father, of which more presently.
The passage is evidently regarded by him as an
amplification of the idea of the term εἰκών, for he
concludes with a brief reference to two other scriptural
expressions used of the Son,—"the radiance of the
glory of God" (Heb. i. 3, ἀπαύγασμα τῆς δόξης τοῦ
Θεοῦ) and "the unstained mirror" (Wisdom of Solomon,
vii. 26, κάτοπτρον ἀκηλίδωτον),—both of which terms,
he says, preserve in a variety of ways the idea of an
image.

Diekamp remarks that the "entrusting" of the
Word with the work of revelation is an echo of the
subordinationism of Origen. The same note is heard
more clearly in the description of the Son as a "standard" of creation (see p. 18). On the other hand the
description of the Son as an ἀπόρροια in the fragment
quoted by Athanasius marks a tendency to Homoousianism which is developed still more clearly in the present
fragment when the writer comes to dwell upon the
likeness of the Son to the Father (see pp. 25 f.). The
mind of Theognostus, like that of Origen, worked
alternately on two lines, "one leading to Arianism, the
other to Homoousianism" (Diekamp, p. 487).

It is instructive to compare this fragment with the
earlier extract from the *Hypotyposeis*. Of the two
descriptions there given of the Son the one (ἀπόρροια)
marked His origin in and His distinctness from the
Father, the other (εἰκὼν) His resemblance to and His

representation of the Father. The same two lines of
thought are patent in the present extract. *Logos*
denotes the Son as the offspring of the Father's mind:
but, as thought is richer than language, *Sophia* is used
to denote the Son as the complete expression of the
Father's mind. The words fall into pairs, as may be
shown by a diagram:

$\lambda \acute{o} \gamma o s$, cp. $\left\{ \begin{array}{l} \dot{a}\pi \acute{o}\rho\rho o\iota a \\ \dot{a}\pi a\acute{v}\gamma a\sigma\mu a \end{array} \right\}$ = origin and distinctness.

$\sigma o\phi \acute{\iota} a$, cp. $\left\{ \begin{array}{l} e\dot{\iota}\kappa \grave{\omega}\nu \\ \kappa \acute{a}\tau o\pi\tau\rho o\nu \end{array} \right\}$ = resemblance and representation.

It may not be too refined a distinction to note that
whereas Origen, working outwards from God to the
world, places *Sophia* first and *Logos* second among the
$\dot{e}\pi \acute{\iota}\nu o\iota a\iota$ of the Son, i.e. "His economic functions, His
relations to the world[1]," Theognostus, who is dealing
with the two terms in the order of their adequacy,
proceeds from the *Logos* which expresses to the *Sophia*
which is expressed. Both denote the Son as the
expression of the Father, but *Logos* looks outward to
man and *Sophia* inward to God.

It will be observed that Theognostus makes "Son"
the personal name of the second hypostasis within the
Godhead; *Logos* and *Sophia* are titles or descriptions
of "the Son." Harnack sees in this an indication of
the way in which the Logos-doctrine of the apologists
had given place to the doctrine of the eternal Sonship,

[1] Bigg, *op. cit.* pp. 168, 169, n. 1.

and the name of Son had passed from the historic
Christ to the preexistent Word. But he is hardly
warranted in thinking that the object of this passage
in Theognostus is to vindicate the use of the terms
Logos and *Sophia* from the neglect or disfavour which
resulted from the prominence of the doctrine of the
Sonship. Theognostus is simply taking one by one the
terms applied to the Son in Scripture and explaining
their respective connotations and their comparative
values. One of the most marked Origenistic features
of the passage is its scriptural basis. Harnack himself
remarks that Theognostus like Origen was " a sturdily
biblical theologian" (*streng biblischer Theologe, T. U.*
p. 89).

6. Theognostus proceeds in the latter part of this
extract to elaborate the idea of resemblance to the
Father which is conveyed by the term εἰκών, and starts
again from the language of the Scriptures. " They say
that in Him dwelleth the fulness of all the Godhead[1].
They mean not that He is one thing, and that the
Godhead is something distinct entering into Him and

[1] Col. ii. 9, ἐν αὐτῷ κατοικεῖ πᾶν τὸ πλήρωμα τῆς θεότητος σωματικῶς.
Theognostus quotes freely, οἰκεῖν τὸ πλ. τῆς θ. πάσης, and omits
σωματικῶς. Diekamp and Harnack both remark upon the application
of this text here, not to the incarnate but to the preexistent Logos,
as though it were a violent use of the text. But Lightfoot and Ellicott
(*ad loc.*) both recognise this application as intended by S. Paul,
though " σωματικῶς is added to show that the Word, in whom the
pleroma thus had its abode from all eternity, crowned His work by
the Incarnation " (Lightfoot).

dwelling in Him, but that He is like the Father in this
respect, that His *ousia* is full, like the *ousia* of the
Father, of all that constitutes God. Having this likeness to the Father in *ousia*, He will have it also in
point of number. Wherefore there is but one Word,
one Wisdom. The Father needed no second Wisdom,
nor was there likely to be in future any other impress[1]
of His *ousia*, as though the first were defective. He
can only have this likeness to the full if it be not
even lacking in point of number also. One Himself,
and retaining in its integrity His likeness to the One[2],
He will thus be unchangeable, being the copy ($\mu i\mu\eta\mu a$)
of the unchangeable Father. That which is completely
inclined to likeness[3] to the One can never experience a
change."

In this elaboration of the $\delta\mu o\iota \delta\tau\eta s$ of Father and
Son there are two points which stand out clearly.
(i) There is the assertion of the *unity* of the Son. By
this Theognostus means the unity of $\dot{a}\rho\iota\theta\mu\delta s$, not the

[1] $\dot{\epsilon}\kappa\mu a\gamma\epsilon\hat{\iota}o\nu$, used lit. (e.g. Plat. *Theaet.* 194 D, E) of an impression
made upon a soft substance. Cp. $\chi a\rho a\kappa\tau\dot{\eta}\rho$ $\tau\hat{\eta}s$ $\dot{\upsilon}\pi o\sigma\tau\dot{a}\sigma\epsilon\omega s$ $a\dot{\upsilon}\tau o\hat{\upsilon}$ (Heb.
i. 2), R.V. "the very image of His substance" (marg. "the impress"),
χ. being lit. the stamp upon a coin or seal.

[2] The context indicates that $\tau o\hat{\upsilon}$ $\dot{\epsilon}\nu\delta s$ is masculine, not neuter like
the Neo-platonist $\tau\dot{o}$ $\ddot{\epsilon}\nu$.

[3] Diekamp remarks upon the homoousian tendency of this passage.
Theognostus uses indeed only the word $\delta\mu o\iota \delta\tau\eta s$ (*Ähnlichkeit*), but it
is an $\delta\mu o\iota \delta\tau\eta s$ which is $\pi\lambda\eta\rho\dot{\eta}s$ and $\dot{a}\kappa\rho\iota\beta\dot{\eta}s$ and practically a *Gleichkeit*,
almost identity. It is the language of "an Origenism advanced some
way further already in the direction of the Nicene formula."

unity of ἕνωσις. He is not thinking of the unity in
complexity which results from or is consistent with the
coexistence of two or more elements in one being (e.g.
the unity of the two natures in the person of the
incarnate Son); he is thinking of the unity of the single
existence of the only thing of its kind,—there is one
Logos and no second. We are again reminded of
Origen, who asserted the unity of the Logos in this
sense on the ground that it was impossible that there
should be more than one objective Truth[1]. (ii) There
is the assertion of the *immutability* of the Son. Here
again is an echo of Origen, who insisted not only on
the unchangeableness of the *ousia* of the Son incarnate,
even while He accommodated Himself to the limitations
of human life (*c. Cels.* iv. 14), but also upon the unchangeableness of the Logos as the εἰκὼν ἀναλλοίωτος
of the Father. Diekamp (*op. cit.* pp. 487, 488) says
that such emphasis upon the unity and immutability
of the Logos is rare indeed in the third century, though
frequent enough afterwards in the conflict with Arianism. He endeavours to prove that Theognostus is here
writing in special opposition to the teaching of Lucian
of Antioch, who held apparently that apart from the
eternal Logos within the Godhead there was a created
Logos who assumed a human body and who appears in
Holy Scripture as the redeemer and as the son of the
heavenly Father. This second Logos was an imperfect

[1] Neander, ii. 308.

image of the Father, being subject to change and attaining to perfection only by progress. This theory of Diekamp's is bound up with the assumption that the present passage is an extract from the seventh book of the *Hypotyposeis* and that this book is a later addition to the work, intended to correct its earlier errors. The theory is rejected by Harnack, who thinks that the emphasis which Theognostus lays here on the unity and immutability of the Logos is sufficiently explained by the fact that Origen himself was accused of "preaching two Christs[1]" by those who misunderstood or misrepresented his "complex Christology" (*T. U.* p. 91). Theognostus may be vindicating here the orthodoxy of Origenist theology; but the hypothesis is superfluous. The points upon which he dwells would come naturally enough in an analysis of the ideas involved in the scriptural designations of the Son. It is unnecessary to postulate any special object of attack or apology in a work which, as far as its fragments serve to indicate, was uncontroversial in character.

7. Of the Christology of Theognostus in the strict sense of the word, i.e. his view of the conditions or consequences of the Incarnation, we have two indications in Photius' comments on the fifth and sixth books (περὶ τῆς ἐνανθρωπήσεως τοῦ Σωτῆρος). Photius notes with approval that in these books Theognostus set

---

[1] Pamphilus, his apologist, says, "asserunt eum duos Christos praedicare" (Routh, *R. S.* iv. 367).

himself, "as his custom was," to prove the possibility of
the Incarnation[1]. This notice recalls his argument in
the second book in proof of the necessity of the divine
Sonship. Theognostus must in a sense be ranked with
the apologists; he can turn from the doctrinal exegesis
of Scripture to the rational justification of Christian
doctrine. It is interesting to find room made thus in
a systematic outline of theology for a philosophical proof
of certain of its presuppositions. This philosophical
element may be due to the influence of Aristotelian
thought and methods; but Harnack is strongly inclined
to see here an anticipation of the conflict between
Christianity and Neo-platonism. The eternity of matter
and the impossibility of a divine Sonship or of an incarnation of deity were among the chief points which
the Neo-platonists maintained so vigorously against the
Church teachers of a later age (*T. U.* p. 83).

The remainder of these two books Photius dismisses
with a general disparagement of their many "inanities,"

[1] *Cod.* 106...ἐπιχειρεῖ μέν, ὡς ἔθος αὐτῷ, τὴν ἐνανθρώπησιν τοῦ υἱοῦ
δυνατὸν εἶναι δεικνύναι, πολλὰ δὲ ἐν αὐτοῖς κενοφωνεῖ καὶ μάλιστα
ὅταν ἀποτολμᾷ λέγειν ὅτι τὸν υἱὸν φανταζόμεθα κ.τ.λ. (see below).
Harnack (*Hist. of Dogma*, E. Tr. iii. 97) says that "the grounds on
which he based the possibility of the Incarnation were empty and
worthless." But Photius does not say this. He is contrasting the
argument in proof of the Incarnation with some of the other contents
of these two books. ἐν αὐτοῖς = "in these books," not "in these
proofs of the Incarnation." Besides, the particular example which
Photius singles out for condemnation is not part of the proof of the
possibility of the Incarnation, but part of the explanation of its
manner or *conditions*.

among which he singles out for special condemnation
the "venturesome assertion" that the personal presence
of the incarnate Son was limited by the time and place
of each appearance, and that it was only His activity
that remained unlimited (ὅτι τὸν υἱὸν φανταζόμεθα
ἄλλοτε ἐν ἄλλοις τόποις περιγραφόμενον, μόνῃ δὲ τῇ
ἐνεργείᾳ μὴ περιγραφόμενον). This idea seems to
belong in some way to the teaching of Origen on the
different appearances of the Saviour in different forms
to different persons according to their powers of appre-
hension[1]. But we have no evidence of the precise
connexion between the two ideas.

8. Two notices remain for our consideration. One
is the brief statement of Photius that Theognostus
represented the Son as exercising authority over
rational beings only (τῶν λογικῶν μόνον ἐπιστατεῖν).
The other is the interesting passage in Athanasius'
fourth letter to Serapion in which he cites Theognostus
and Origen as both interpreting the unpardonable sin
of blasphemy against the Holy Spirit to mean the sin
of the baptized, who alike in knowledge and in grace
stand in a special relation to the Holy Spirit. These
two questions are closely connected as parts of a wider
question, viz. the question of distinctions of external
function within the Holy Trinity. In the New
Testament we find the idea of such distinctive functions

[1] Bull, *Def. Fid. Nic.* i. 293, 301; Routh, *R. S.* iii. 420; Hagenbach, *Hist. of Doctr.* (E. Tr.), i. 247, 248.

side by side with the idea of the unity of all action of
the Trinity. The attributes or operations assigned
there to the three Persons respectively may fairly be
summed up under the familiar categories of creation,
redemption and sanctification. But they are not
regarded as mutually exclusive. The language of some
of the passages implies that the action of the Son and
of the Spirit is embraced within the action of the
Father (e.g. 1 Cor. xii. 4 f., Eph. iv. 4-6). Other
passages indicate that in each of the three stages of
human destiny,—creation, redemption, sanctification,—
each of the divine Persons has a share. Nowhere is
there a suggestion that the sphere of action of the Son
or of the Spirit is less extensive than that of the
Father. It was Origen who drew this inference, and
stated it with an emphasis which outweighed the safer
side of his teaching and gave an obvious ground of
attack for later critics to seize. Justinian in his letter
to Mennas in 553 quotes Origen as saying: "God the
Father, embracing all things, extends to each of the
things that exist, imparting to each of them existence
from His own, for He is self-existent. The Son is inferior to the Father, extending only to rational beings,
for He is second to the Father. The Holy Spirit is still
less, penetrating only to the holy. So in this respect the
power of the Father is greater than that of the Son
and the Holy Spirit, and the power of the Son than
that of the Holy Spirit, and the power of the Spirit

again is superior to all other holy things." Photius echoes this statement. Origen, he says, taught that "the Father pervades all things that exist, while the Son extends only to rational beings, and the Spirit only to the saved." Jerome conveys the same idea of Origen's teaching (*Ep.* 94 *ad Avitum*). For anything more than fragments of the original Greek of the *De Principiis* we are dependent upon the translation made by Rufinus, in which we cannot be sure that we have always a faithful representation of the actual language of Origen. Roughly speaking, however, in ch. iii. of the first book of the *De Principiis* Origen seems to mark a difference of extent as well as of character in the action of each Person. He distinguishes their functions as well as their spheres of action. But he explains this differentiation in language which shows that the spheres of action are determined, not by varying degrees of power or dignity within the Godhead, but by the capacity of the objects of the different operations, and by the character of the gifts bestowed by those operations. The Father bestows existence, the Son reason, the Spirit holiness[1]. Origen endeavours indeed to safeguard the truth of the unity of all operations of the Holy Trinity. There is the unity of source; e.g. he writes

[1] In the catechisms of later ages of the Church it is the redemption of sinful humanity which is singled out as the special work of the Son; in Origen it is the endowment of humanity with intelligence and knowledge. It is the eternal Word on whose function Origen lays stress rather than the incarnate Saviour.

" what is called the gift of the Spirit is revealed through
the Son and wrought through the Father," i.e. there is
one stream of action descending from God to man
through the Son and the Spirit. There is also the
unity of purpose. The stream descends to ascend again
to its source. The holiness given by the Spirit brings
capacity for a further revelation of Christ the Word as
being also the righteousness of God, and thus man is
led nearer to the realisation of his destined likeness to
God. Still there were two features in this view of
Origen's which gave serious offence.

(a) There was the rigid demarcation of the three
spheres of operation,—the universe, humanity, the
Church. Athanasius suggested that perhaps the language of Origen and Theognostus did not mean exactly
what it said; and Huet in his *Origeniana* and Bishop
Bull in his *Defensio Fidei Nicaenae* (i. 379, 380) held
that what Origen meant was merely such distinctive
functions as are compatible with the common action of
all three Persons. M. Denis in his *Philosophie d'Origène*
(p. 122) interprets the offending passage of the *De
Principiis* in the light of a reference in Origen's *Contra
Celsum* (vi. 65) to the words of S. Paul in Rom. xi. 36,
ἐξ αὐτοῦ καὶ δι' αὐτοῦ καὶ εἰς αὐτὸν τὰ πάντα, which
Origen explains there as denoting the origin (ἀρχήν),
the control (συνοχήν), the destiny (τέλος) of all created
existence. " Le partage du Père, c'est la création, en
tant qu'il est le principe de l'être de toutes choses ; celui

du Fils, quoiqu'il soit créateur en ce sens que tout a été
fait par son ministère, c'est le gouvernement des choses
temporelles, ou ce qu'Origène appelle l'économie divine ;
celui du Saint-Esprit, c'est la sanctification, fin dernière
de l'œuvre de la Trinité ; de sorte que l'action une et
diverse de Dieu est marquée dans les trois moments
principaux par les termes de Père (ἐξ αὐτοῦ), de Fils
(δι' αὐτοῦ), de Saint-Esprit (εἰς αὐτόν)." The language
of M. Denis verges on Sabellianism, but his meaning
is clear. He drops the idea of separate spheres of
operation, and takes Origen as intending only to dis-
tinguish the functions, not to restrict the action, of the
Persons. Redepenning on the other hand stands by
the idea of these "concentric spheres"; but he points
out,—and here M. Denis follows him,—that the circum-
ferences of these circles are unequal only during the
process of the world's development, and coincide in the
final stage of its evolution. For Origen the non-rational
has no essential and therefore eternal being. It merely
subserves the ends of the rational. It was not at the
first, and will not be at the last. The rational on the
other hand will become the spiritual. "We think,"
says Origen (Rufin. *De Princ.* ii. 202), "that every
rational creature attains to participation in the Spirit
as well as to participation in the wisdom of God and
the Word without any difference." In that distant
future the sphere of the Son and the sphere of the
Spirit will be one and the same with the sphere of the

Father; and the only dissimilarity then remaining between Son and Spirit will be their difference in point
of relation to the Father. At present the Son reigns
over the unintelligent and carnal as Shepherd; over
those who understand the meaning of the visible world
He reigns as the Christ who lifts them through His
earthly appearance to the invisible and heavenly world;
over those who rise already to the recognition of the
invisible He reigns as King and Only-begotten in His
Divinity. At present the kingdom of Christ is a
kingdom in process; it is the stage of growth in knowledge and in righteousness. The "kingdom of God" is
as yet only an inner circle of light and peace in the
Holy Spirit within the kingdom of Christ. But when
the Son shall be as completely subject to the Father in
the person of the members of His Body as He is
already in Himself, then His kingdom shall come to an
end, and God shall be all in all (Redep. ii. 307).

(b) The second difficulty arises from Origen's
assertion in this fragment that there are diminishing
degrees of power and dignity,—the Son being inferior
to the Father, and the Spirit to the Father and the
Son, on the ground of the limitation of the range of
their respective activities. This assertion is one side of
the subordinationism of Origen, the other side being the
inferiority in point of relation to the Father. Photius
seems to have brought a similar charge against Pierius,
whom he accuses of saying that the Spirit was inferior

in glory (δόξα) to the Father and the Son (see p. 52).
Still perhaps we may safely appeal here from Origen to
Origen in his own defence, if Rufinus is to be trusted.
Rufinus makes him say, "nihil in Trinitate majus
minusve dicendum est"; and the saying can scarcely be
restricted to the essential Trinity, for it comes in a
context where Origen is expressly dealing with this
very question of the external revelation of the Trinity
in grace and truth.

  The difficulty however that gave most trouble to
Origen and to Theognostus arose from the fact that
their theory had two opposite results. If on the one
hand the limited extent of the operation of the Spirit
seemed to them logically to involve the inferiority
of the Spirit, even while they went on stating the
equality of the Persons, on the other hand the fact
that the "saints" to whom they limited the work of the
Spirit are the highest order in God's world seemed as
logically to require them to rank the Spirit as highest
in dignity within the Trinity. Origen and Theognostus
both repudiate this conclusion with an anxiety which
shows that they felt its apparent force. Origen deals
with the question in connexion with our Lord's saying
that blasphemy against the Son of Man was pardonable,
but blasphemy against the Holy Spirit unpardonable.
A rational being, he says, who ceases to live in the light
of reason is deserving of pardon because his fall is as
much the result as the cause of ignorance or folly.

But a relapse after receiving the grace of the Spirit is resistance offered to the Spirit. " Yet let no one think that because we have said that the Holy Spirit is bestowed upon the holy alone, while the blessings and operations of the Father and the Son reach good and bad alike, we have therefore placed the Spirit above the Father and the Son, or thereby claim for Him a greater dignity. That is a most unwarrantable conclusion. We have merely been describing the special character of His grace and work. *Nihil in Trinitate majus minusve dicendum est.*" It is throughout the Father who controls by His Word and sanctifies by His Spirit.

Theognostus felt the force of this difficulty even more than Origen, to judge from the two fragments of the later writer which Athanasius has preserved in his reply to Serapion's enquiry about this very question of the sin of blasphemy against the Holy Spirit. Athanasius says (*Ep.* 4 *ad Serap.* c. xi.) that both Origen and Theognostus,—he had consulted their writings[1] on the

---

[1] τούτων γὰρ τοῖς περὶ τούτων συνταγματίοις ἐνέτυχον, ὅτε τὴν ἐπι-στολὴν ἔγραψας. (a) Harnack (*Altchr. Litt.* i. 437) thinks that these συνταγμάτια were separate treatises dealing with the sin in question. But Bardenhewer (*Altk. Litt.* ii. 198) points out that the writing of Origen here quoted was only a chapter of the *De Principiis,* and that probably therefore the writing of Theognostus was similarly an extract from the *Hypotyposeis,* perhaps from the third book. That book, as we have seen, dealt with the Holy Spirit, and its teaching is compared by Photius to the teaching of the *De Principiis.* (b) Harnack (*T. U.* p. 84) translates ἐνέτυχον "auf diese Schriftchen *gestossen* sei," i.e. " had only just come across these writings," whereas the larger

subject after receiving Serapion's enquiry,—were agreed
that the blasphemy in question was the sin of relapse
in those who had received the baptismal gift of the
Spirit.   They referred (or it may be Athanasius who
refers) to Heb. iv. 4 foll. for the impossibility of restoring
the enlightened who fell back into sin.   Theognostus,
he adds, proceeded to define three stages or standards
($ὅροι$)[1] which are transgressed by different kinds of sin.
" He who has transgressed the first stage and the second
might be deemed worthy of a less punishment; but he
who despised the third also would no longer find pardon."
The first and second $ὅροι$, which are coupled without
any note of distinction, Athanasius explains to be the
teaching that relates to the Father and the Son ; the
third is the teaching given to Christians at their
initiation ($τελειώσει$) and their participation in the gift
of the Spirit, i.e. at the time of their baptism.   Theognostus, he tells us, refers at this point to the Lord's

works of both Origen and Theognostus must have been long familiar to
Athanasius.   But $ἐντυγχάνειν$ = (1) to meet with, (2) to *read*.   Routh
(*R.S.* iii. 416) translates "horum opera *legebam* cum epistolam accepi."
But the aorist $ἐνέτυχον$ suggests that Athanasius consulted the writings
on receiving Serapion's letter.

[1] Four ideas of "definition" seem to be combined here in $ὅρος$,
(1) the *range of authority* exercised by Father, Son and Spirit respectively, (2) the *extent of the teaching* received by the different classes of
believers from or concerning the Son and the Spirit, (3) the *rule of
life* laid down by the teaching, (4) the *class* or *category* in which the
recipients of the teaching are thereby placed.   (2) is the most obvious
meaning here, and is evidently the sense intended by Athanasius; but
the first and third seem to be implied also by Theognostus.

promise (John xvi. 12, 13) that the Spirit should give
the disciples the teaching which they were not yet able
to receive from Himself. Then follows the extract from
Theognostus in which he turns to face the difficulty
which seems to be involved in this idea of the sin against
the Spirit as the worst of all sins. " The Saviour holds
converse with those who cannot yet receive perfect
teaching, condescending to their weakness, while the
Holy Spirit dwells with those who are being perfected[1].
Yet the teaching of the Spirit cannot be described as
superior on that account to the teaching of the Son.
We can only say that the Son condescends to the
imperfect ($\dot{\alpha}\tau\epsilon\lambda\dot{\epsilon}\sigma\iota\nu$), while the Spirit is the seal of
those who are being perfected ($\tau\epsilon\lambda\epsilon\iota\upsilon\mu\dot{\epsilon}\nu\omega\nu$). So it is

---

[1] $\sigma\upsilon\gamma\gamma\dot{\iota}\nu\epsilon\tau\alpha\iota$ $\tau\hat{o}\hat{\iota}s$ $\tau\epsilon\lambda\epsilon\iota\upsilon\mu\dot{\epsilon}\nu\upsilon\iota s$. (1) In patristic writings $\tau\dot{\epsilon}\lambda\epsilon\iota\upsilon s$ is
used of " the baptized believer admitted to the full privileges of the
Christian life," $\tau\epsilon\lambda\epsilon\iota\upsilon\hat{\upsilon}\nu$ of the administration of baptism, and
$\tau\epsilon\lambda\epsilon\dot{\iota}\omega\sigma\iota s$ of the baptism itself. See Westcott, add. note to Heb. ii. 10.
This seems to be the meaning both of $\tau\epsilon\lambda\epsilon\iota\omega\theta\epsilon\hat{\iota}\sigma\iota\nu$ in Theognostus
and of $\tau\epsilon\lambda\epsilon\iota\dot{\omega}\sigma\epsilon\iota$ in Athanasius. The second and third $\ddot{\upsilon}\rho\upsilon\iota$ seem thus
to be the state of the catechumen who is awaiting and the state of
the Christian who has received the baptismal gift of the Spirit. (2) But
the present $\tau\epsilon\lambda\epsilon\iota\upsilon\dot{\upsilon}\mu\epsilon\nu\upsilon\iota$ here indicates progress, " being brought to
perfection." These are the Christians who are at once more
advanced and still advancing to higher knowledge. The Alexandrian
school tended to make a separate class of $\tau\epsilon\lambda\epsilon\hat{\iota}\upsilon\iota$ within the baptized,
a class of Christians who were $\tau\epsilon\lambda\epsilon\hat{\iota}\upsilon\iota$ compared with the rest of the
baptized who were still in point of Christian knowledge $\dot{\alpha}\tau\epsilon\lambda\epsilon\hat{\iota}s$. Cp.
Routh, R. S. iii. 416, 417, "peritiorum Christianorum, non baptiza-
torum solum."

not on account of any superiority of the Spirit over
the Son that the blasphemy against the Spirit means a
guilt from which there is no escape and no pardon,—it
is so because while for the imperfect there is yet
forgiveness, for those who tasted the heavenly gift and
were perfected (τελειωθεῖσιν) there remains no excuse
or plea for pardon." The difference lies not in the
varying dignity of the divine Teachers but in the
varying progress of the taught. The unpardonable
character of the blasphemy is due not to any superiority
of the Spirit over the Son, but to the higher endowment
and therefore greater responsibility of those who have
tasted of the heavenly gift. It is not quite clear
whether this gift is the spiritual gift of grace or the
intellectual gift of truth. The general tendency of
Alexandrian theology favours the latter view. It is
then still uncertain whether the teacher is the Spirit
"enabling with perpetual light the dullness of our
blinded sight" or the Church imparting further instruction to the baptized and confirmed. The context
seems to indicate that it is the teaching office of the
Spirit, not the catechetical system of the Church, which
is here in the mind of Theognostus. In that case it is
evident that the difficulty is only pushed a step further
back. As Harnack remarks, teaching for the advanced
disciple seems necessarily higher than teaching for the
imperfect; and it is a natural inference to think that

the teacher who gives the higher teaching must himself rank higher too. Theognostus, like Origen before him, certainly makes it plain that he did not himself regard the Spirit as superior to the Son ; but he does not succeed in removing the objection that his teaching seemed to involve some such superiority. The difficulty was in a sense self-made ; it was the result of too rigid a classification of divine operations, in forgetfulness of the two principles which neither Origen nor Theognostus would for one moment have denied, and which Origen in fact asserted elsewhere, viz. the divinity of both Son and Spirit, and the unity of all operation of the Godhead. As a matter of fact, subsequent theologians dropped these over-logical refinements upon the subject of distinctive functions within the Holy Trinity. Athanasius himself makes a significant change in this very passage. Theognostus had spoken of the teaching of the Spirit and of the Son (τὴν τοῦ πνεύματος διδασκαλίαν ὑπερβάλλειν τῆς τοῦ υἱοῦ διδαχῆς), evidently regarding the Spirit and the Son as the teachers of the Christian converts. Athanasius in his own remarks upon this passage explains the first and second ὅροι of Theognostus as meaning the instruction *concerning* the Father and the Son (τὴν περὶ πατρὸς καὶ υἱοῦ κατήχησιν), and the third as meaning the teaching given to the believer at his baptism (τὸν ἐπὶ τῇ τελειώσει καὶ τῇ τοῦ πνεύματος μετοχῇ παραδιδόμενον λόγον); i.e. he substitutes for the teaching office of the Spirit the catechetical work of the Church. It is no longer a question of comparison between two divine Teachers but merely of comparison between two successive stages of an ecclesiastical system of instruction. The idea of three concentric spheres of operation assigned to different persons of the Holy Trinity was in fact seen to involve a weakness and a danger which led to the practical abandonment of the idea. Later patristic teaching laid stress instead on other aspects of the distinctions within the action of the Godhead. Some of these aspects are indeed internal rather than external. Such for example is the distinction which Hilary drew between the attributes of the three Persons,—*aeternitas in patre, species in imagine, usus in munere.* Such again is that distinction of Augustine's which regards the Father as unity, the Son as equality, and the Spirit as the bond of unity and equality, or that other distinction of his which attributes power to the Father, wisdom to the Son, and goodness to the Spirit. But even where the distinctions drawn are concerned with the operations rather than with the attributes, there are two points to notice. The first is that the operation assigned to the Son is not revelation so much as redemption. In Origen He is the Word enlightening all rational beings; in the later fathers He is the Saviour redeeming sinful souls. Creation, redemption, sanctification,—the point of view has become soteriological. The second point is that the statement of distinct functions is almost always qualified by the recognition of the truth that the operation of the Holy Trinity is one and indivisible,—that neither Son nor Spirit works alone or apart from the Father. The action of each Person is the action of God.

PIERIUS.

WE know more of the life and work of Pierius than
of Theognostus, but the fragments of his writings and
teaching which have survived are even more rare and
disconnected than those which enable us to reconstruct
the theology of Theognostus. From Eusebius[1] we learn
that he was a presbyter of the Alexandrian church
under Theonas (bishop 281/2—300), and was distinguished alike as an ascetic, as a teacher and as a
preacher. Eusebius speaks of his "investigation and
elucidation of divine things" as well as of his addresses
"before the body of the Church"; and Jerome[2]
similarly implies the teacher as distinct from the
preacher when he refers to the skill of Pierius in
dialectic and rhetoric. There is no ground therefore
for doubting the statement of Philippus Sidetes, who
is the first writer to describe Pierius as head of the
catechetical school of Alexandria[3]. His end however

---

[1] *Hist. Eccl.* vii. 32.

[2] *De viris illustr.* 76, p. 166.

[3] See note on the succession of catechists, pp. 1, 2.

is lost in uncertainty. Philippus[1] quotes a poem
written by an Alexandrian advocate named Theodorus
as his authority for saying that Pierius and his brother
became martyrs (ἐμαρτύρησαν), and had a large church
built in their memory at Alexandria; and Photius too
says (*Cod.* 118) that they were " counted worthy of the
crown of the athlete" and that the faithful built a
church and houses in their honour. Eusebius on the
other hand is silent on this point, while Jerome says
that "after the persecution Pierius lived all his life at
Rome." It is possible of course that Philippus and
Photius have confused our Pierius with another Pierius
who did meet with a martyr's death. But it is more
probable that the Alexandrian poet used the word
ἐμαρτύρησαν in the earlier and wider sense of a con-
fessorship involving suffering of any degree. Pierius
may have lived at Rome as a refugee or an exile, driven
from Alexandria in consequence of his activity as a
Christian teacher. The dedication of a church in his
name is not a certain proof of a martyr's death; if the
Dionysius and the Theonas whose churches at Alexandria
are mentioned by Epiphanius were the well-known
bishops of the third century, it is evident that confessors
as well as martyrs in the strict sense of the word were

[1] De Boor in *Texte u. Untersuch.* v. 2. 165–184 (1888) has edited
various new fragments and notices of Pierius (as also of Papias and
Hegesippus) contained in previously unknown excerpts made from
Philippus Sidetes by a late compiler.

commemorated in this way[1]. Pierius was in any case still living in 309. That was the year of the martyrdom of Pamphilus the scholar-priest of Caesarea, who had been a pupil of Pierius at Alexandria; and his old master paid him the tribute of writing his life[2].

It is difficult to determine how many works of Pierius are represented by the quotations and references which have survived. Photius speaks of a book ($\beta\iota\beta\lambda\iota o\nu$) of twelve treatises or sermons ($\lambda\acute{o}\gamma o\iota$). He criticizes their theology with mingled censure and excuse, as we shall see, but gives their style unstinted praise. Their language was clear and plain, flowing without a sign of labour but with all the smoothness and ease of the utterance of the moment, and it was remarkably rich in thought. Unfortunately Photius gives no account of the contents of the volume. He mentions two $\lambda\acute{o}\gamma o\iota$, one entitled "*On the Gospel according to Luke*," and containing a reference to the use of images, and the other bearing the double title "*On Easter and Hosea*," and containing a discussion of the Cherubim of the Tabernacle and the pillar of Jacob. It seems clear that these were two of the twelve, but the other ten are left without a name. Besides the account of Photius we have the authority

[1] De Boor, *op. cit.* pp. 179, 180; Routh, *R. S.* iii. 426; Bardenhewer, *Altk. Litt.* ii. 198, 199; Harnack, *Chron.* ii. 67. Prof. Burkitt has called my attention to a reference to the church of Theonas also in Athan. *de Fuga* 24, quoted in *Dict. Chr. Biogr.*, p. 193.

[2] Phil. Sid. *fr.* 7 in De Boor, p. 171.

of Philippus Sidetes for the following fragments or notices of Pierius: (1) a statement about S. Paul's wife from the "first of the Easter sermons," (2) a bare mention of "many other important works, especially that on the *Theotokos* and that on the beginning of Hosea," (3) a reference to his sermon or treatise (λόγος) on the life of Pamphilus, and (4) an incidental scrap of etymological explanation of Biblical names "according to Pierius." Jerome[1] quotes Pierius as commenting on S. Paul's view of marriage in 1 Cor. vii. 7. These are the data. The problem is to put them into their proper relation to each other[2]. They may all belong to the volume which Photius knew. Harnack thinks that the collection of λόγοι came into the hands of Photius without a general title. The only two that Photius names are, it is true, far enough apart in title to justify our regarding the collection as miscellaneous. On the other hand the use of images and the character of the cherubim are topics cognate enough to suggest a connexion between the discourses in which they occur. Was the volume a collection of Easter sermons on various subjects? Another question that cannot be answered is whether Jerome is citing a sermon or a commentary. The point at issue, viz. S. Paul's view of marriage, seems to indicate that Jerome is referring to that "first of the Easter sermons" from which Philippus

---

[1] *Ep.* 2 *ad Pammach.* (Routh, *R. S.* iii. 429).

[2] Harnack, *Chron.* ii. 68, 69; Bardenhewer, ii. 200–202.

quotes the statement about S. Paul's wife. On the
other hand commentaries by Pierius are mentioned
along with those of Origen by Palladius in his *Historia
Lausiaca* (c. 55)[1]; Palladius tells us that Silvania, a
Christian lady of high rank who came from Jerusalem
to Alexandria about the end of the 4th century, was a
great student of Church literature, and had read and
read time after time various works of Origen, Gregory,
Stephanus, Pierius, Basil and others. The etymological
fragment moreover dealing with the names Herod,
Herodias and Philip seems likely to have come from a
commentary rather than from a sermon, unless indeed
we may go further and credit Pierius with the production of an Onomasticon. It is not a bold conjecture in
the face of Jerome's reference to the *exemplaria* of
Origen and Pierius. If Pierius edited or annotated
MSS. of the New Testament, he may well have com-
piled a glossary.

Pierius was called "Origen the younger[2]." Harnack[3]
used this fact to prove the Origenistic tenor of his
teaching; but it is plain from Jerome, our authority
for this designation, that what gave Pierius this
distinction was the high merit of his treatises and
sermons. None the less it is true in another sense.

[1] Dom Butler, *Hist. Laus.* (*Texts and Studies*, vol. vi.) ii. p. 149
(Migne, *P. G.* xxxiv. 1244) and note 99, on p. 229.

[2] Jerome, *De Vir. Ill.* 76: ut Origenes junior vocaretur.

[3] *Hist. of Dogma*, E. Tr. iii. 96.

Pierius recalled the extravagance as well as the excellence of Origen's work as a teacher. Photius indeed only once compares him in so many words to Origen. Pierius, he says, talks mysteriously about the pre-existence of souls just in Origen's absurd fashion[1]. But the few scattered fragments of his works that remain and the references of Photius to the contents of other works go far to prove that he was a close follower as well as a not unworthy successor of Origen. Harnack is probably right in suggesting that it was from Pierius that Pamphilus "inherited his unconditional devotion" to Origen's theology[2].

Palladius says (*Hist. Laus.* c. 11)[3] that Ammonius the Tall, the famous Egyptian monk, knew by heart large portions of the writings of Origen, Didymus, Stephanus and Pierius, and that Silvania had studied the commentaries of Origen and Pierius (ib. c. 55). This collocation of the two is borne out in various ways. Jerome remarks on Matt. xxiv. 36 that the words "neque filius" found in some Latin texts of that chapter were absent from the Greek, and in particular from "the manuscripts (*exemplaria*) of Adamantius and Pierius." Harnack[4] understands this to mean not

---

[1] *Cod.* 119, ὑπαινίττεται δὲ οὗτος, κατὰ τὸν Ὠριγένους ὕθλον, καὶ προϋπαρξιν ψυχῶν.

[2] *Hist. of Dogma*, E. Tr. iii. 96.

[3] Butler, *op. cit.* ii. p. 34 (Migne, *P. G.* xxxiv. 1034) and n. 21 on p. 191.

[4] *Altchr. Litt.* i. 439.

merely copies made by them but texts revised or
annotated by them. Jerome had probably observed
such at Caesarea, the scene of the labours of Pamphilus,
who may have brought the MSS. from Alexandria.
Like Origen again, Pierius was strong in exegesis also.
It is true that the strange derivations which he gives
of the names Philip, Herod and Herodias, whether
excerpts from a word-book or from a commentary or
from a sermon, mark indeed the limits of his scholar-
ship; Harnack aptly remarks that they "show that he
made an attempt at Hebrew, and that poor enough[1]."
But his exegetical worth seems to have made an
impression on readers of the fourth century; and
Philippus notes expressly that in his life of Pamphilus
he made a helpful contribution to the study of Holy
Scripture[2]. Here is perhaps the explanation of the
silence of Eusebius on the subject of this memoir.
That silence has been attributed "to the literary rivalry

---

[1] *Chron.* ii. 69, n. 1. Bardenhewer (ii. 202) suggests that as the
three names come together in Matt. xiv. 3 and Mark vi. 17, these
derivations may have occurred in a sermon of Pierius on the death of
the Baptist. This suggestion is not precluded by the fact that they are
attached by Philippus Sidetes to a notice of Philip the deacon. The
fragment runs as follows: Φίλιππος στόμα λαμπάδων. Ἡρωδίας ἀπατω-
μένη. Ἡρώδης δερματίνη δόξα κατὰ Πιέριον. Bardenhewer points out
that this derivation of Herod passed into various Greek and Latin
onomastica (e.g. Jerome, "Erodes pellis gloria"), though it is obviously
an entire mistake, Ἡρώδης being a contraction of the Greek patronymic
Ἡρωΐδης.

[2] De Boor, p. 171, πλεῖστα ὠφέλησεν ἐν τῇ θείᾳ γραφῇ.

of the author of another life of Pamphilus[1]"; but it
is much more intelligible if the writing in question
was a sermon in which Pierius dealt very little with
Pamphilus and very much with exegesis or the study
of Scripture[2].

But it was not only in the direction in which he
laboured that Pierius resembled Origen. His teaching
itself was Origenistic in content and in tone. His
language in reference to the Father and the Son, Photius
tells us, was "reverent" (i.e. orthodox). There was one
exception. He spoke of two οὐσίαι and two φύσεις.
Photius qualifies this criticism by remarking that the
context proved that Pierius was using these terms as
equivalent to ὑποστάσεις and not in the Arian sense.
It was merely, as we should say, an example of the
vague and yet undefined terminology of an age which
had not yet seen the necessity of choosing carefully and
fixing rigidly its doctrinal vocabulary. As Photius
himself noted in a previous sentence, much of the language of Pierius lay outside the later definitions of the
Church[3]. It was in a sense "archaic" (ἀρχαιοτρόπως),
i.e. it belonged to an age before the great heresies which
led the Church to define its statements of doctrine. But,

[1] De Boor, p. 181.

[2] Harnack, *Chron.* ii. 69.

[3] *Cod.* 119, πολλὰ δὲ ἔξω τῶν νῦν ἐν τῇ ἐκκλησίᾳ καθεστηκότων,
ἀρχαιοτρόπως ἴσως, ἀποφαίνεται. For examples of the varying use of
doctrinal terms in pre-Arian writers, see Newman, *Arians of the 4th
cent.*, p. 452.

Photius proceeds, on the subject of the Spirit Pierius
was unorthodox and extremely dangerous, for he asserted
that the Spirit was inferior in glory to the Father and
the Son[1]. This expression may be a quotation from
Pierius or a summary of his teaching. It is insufficient
alone to explain what is intended by the inferiority of
the Spirit. Prof. Swete in his *Early History of the
Doctrine of the Holy Spirit* (p. 25) suggests that Pierius
"approached singularly near to those of the semi-Arian
party who holding the deity of the Son hesitated to
give the like honour to the Holy Ghost. Yet the
disciple of Origen did not go the length of calling
the Divine Spirit a creature like the disciples of Arius
and Macedonius." In his *History of the Doctrine of
the Procession of the Holy Spirit* (p. 66) he suggests
that Photius means that "Pierius like Origen asserted
the production, that is the procession, of the Holy
Ghost from the Father through the Son." To these
two inferiorities of essence and origin we may add a
third, the inferiority of office. Origen was accused of
making the Spirit inferior to the Father and the Son
by limiting His sphere of action to the faithful, just as
he limited the sphere of action of the Son to rational
beings. Pierius may have shared this error, as Theognostus did.

In his Easter sermon on Hosea Pierius dealt with

[1] *Cod.* ὑποβεβηκέναι γὰρ αὐτὸ (i.e. τὸ Πνεῦμα) τῆς τοῦ Πατρὸς καὶ Υἱοῦ
ἀποφάσκει δόξης.

the cherubim which Moses made and with the pillar of
Jacob. He acknowledged the historical fact of their
being made, but offered an explanation which Photius
describes as absurd, viz. that they were a concession of
the divine "economy[1]." It is not clear whether Pierius
meant (a) that the cherubim themselves were permitted
as an immature stage in the development of worship,
or (b) that the parts of Holy Scripture relating to the
cherubim were permitted for the purpose of "economi-
cal," i.e. allegorical, interpretation by later ages. The
latter rendering would bring the words of Pierius into
line with the allegorism of Origen, who interpreted the
cherubim in Isaiah's vision of the throne of God as
indicating the Logos and the Holy Ghost[2]. The former
rendering seems more in accordance with the concluding
remarks of Photius[3], which apparently mean that
Pierius described the images not as representing any
type of creature actually existing, but as merely bearing
the semblance of wings, i.e. they were not real beings
but obviously symbolic figures, not creatures likely to
be idolised in the strict sense of the word, but ideas

---

[1] *Cod.* τὴν μὲν ποίησιν αὐτῶν ὁμολογεῖ, οἰκονομίας δὲ λόγῳ συγχωρη-
θῆναι ματαιολογεῖ.

[2] *Comm. in Rom.* iii. 515; see Redepenning, *Origenes*, ii. 389, n. 1.

[3] *Cod.* 119, ὡς οὐδὲν ἦσαν ὡς ἕτερα τὰ γεγενημένα· οὐδὲ τύπον ἄλλον
ἔφερε μορφῆς ἀλλὰ μόνον πτερύγων κενολογεῖ φέρειν αὐτὰ σχῆμα (Routh,
R. S. iii. 431, with notes on pp. 434, 435). Bardenhewer gives up the
text as hopelessly corrupt. But the general meaning seems clear from
the antithesis of μορφὴ and σχῆμα.

visualised as a help to the worship of God. With
regard to the pillar of Jacob Photius gives us no
information at all of what Pierius wrote.

It was natural that the patriarch of the Greek
Church upon whom fell the last reverberations of the
storm of the iconoclastic controversy should note
another passage of Pierius which bore upon the use of
images in Christian worship. In the sermon on the
Gospel of S. Luke Pierius said what practically amounted
to the argument that the honour or dishonour of an
eikon is the honour or dishonour of its prototype or
original[1]. In the absence of all context this might have
been taken to refer to the honouring of Christ as the
image of the Father (John v. 23), or to the honouring
of human nature as the image of God. But the
circumstances of the age which preceded the days of

[1] *Cod.* 119, ἔχει δὲ χρῆσιν εἰς τὸν λόγον οὗ ἡ ἐπιγραφὴ Εἰς τὸ κατὰ
Λουκᾶν, δι᾽ ἧς ἔστι παριστᾶν ὅτι ἡ τῆς εἰκόνος τιμὴ καὶ ἀτιμία τοῦ πρωτο-
τύπου ἐστὶ τιμὴ ἢ πάλιν ἀτιμία. Tixeront, *Théologie ante-nicéenne*,
p. 415: "un témoignage en faveur du culte des images." It is
perhaps doubtful whether Pierius can be claimed as directly ap-
proving the use of images. The question had not arisen in his day.
If it had, his Origenistic sympathies would probably have led him to
deprecate images of Christ, as Eusebius of Caesarea did in the next
century, on the ground that the human nature of Christ had been
sublimated into the divine. His allegorical interpretation of the
cherubim makes it improbable that he would approve the use of
images; and the language of Photius might be satisfied by the
supposition that he found in Pierius a remark, perhaps in some other
connexion, which seemed to him capable of employment as an
argument in favour of the principle on which the use of images was
justified by its defenders.

Photius and the fact that Photius mentions this passage
in juxtaposition with the passage about the cherubim
make it certain that he took the words of Pierius to
have a bearing upon the reverence due to images in
the Christian church. The dictum which he attributes
to Pierius, or which perhaps he regards as a proper
inference from the language of Pierius, recalls the
argument of Theodore of the Studium in the eighth
century, who said, " the worship of the image is worship
of Christ, because the image is what it is in virtue of
its likeness to Christ." "The theologians demanded
the preservation and worship,—reverence rather than
worship in the modern English use of the words,—of the
icons as a security for the remembrance of the Manhood
of the Lord[1]."

Jerome says that Pierius in his exposition of 1 Cor.
vii. 7 remarked: "In saying this, Paul preaches celibacy
outright[2]." It is interesting therefore to find Philippus
stating that in the first of his paschal sermons Pierius
insisted strenuously that " Paul had a wife and dedi-
cated her to the service of God in the Church, ceasing
to live with her[3]." De Boor sees in this statement a
way of escape which Pierius found for himself out of
the dilemma between S. Paul's language in 1 Cor. vii. 7

---

[1] W. H. Hutton, *The Church and the Barbarians*, p. 164.

[2] *Ep.* 2 *ad Pammach.* ταῦτα λέγων Παῦλος ἀντικρὺς ἀγαμίαν
κηρύσσει.

[3] De Boor, pp. 170, 180.

and the tradition of the early Church that he was married. If Pierius is right in his statement, S. Paul might well have penned that otherwise perplexing wish, for he was in that case practically ἄγαμος. It is a matter of minor interest to speculate on the identity of the writings from which Jerome and Philippus quote. Philippus mentions the sermon " on the beginning of Hosea" separately from the first of the paschal sermons. Otherwise it would be tempting to identify the two sermons, as Harnack does. We might then readily suppose that the strange marriage of Hosea, with its divine counterpart in the relations between God and His chosen people, had been taken by Pierius as a starting-point for an exposition of the place of marriage in the Christian life.

Of the λόγος περὶ τῆς Θεοτόκου we have only the title so quoted by Philippus. If the title came in that shape from the pen of Pierius, it would be the earliest example of the use of the expression θεότοκος by itself. But although the Blessed Virgin was certainly described as " Mother of God " a hundred years before the title became a battle-cry in the Nestorian conflict, yet it is improbable that the title was already in such general use as to stand by itself as a proper name in the heading of a treatise[1]. The treatise or sermon of

[1] In all the cases where the word occurs in the fragments of Alexander, bishop of Alexandria 311 ?–326 (Pitra, *A. S.* iv. 434), it is an epithet attached to the name Mary,—it never stands alone. It

Pierius may have borne the name of the Blessed Virgin, and probably was a treatise on the fact of the Incarnation and in particular on its method, the Virgin Birth; but the title of the writing as it stands is perhaps due to the compiler who lived in the midst of the conflict over the doctrinal issues involved in calling or in refusing to call the Blessed Virgin "Mother of God."

always comes moreover in a context which tones down the sharpness of the expression.

PETER THE MARTYR.

THE tide of Origenistic thought and influence at Alexandria rose to its height with Pierius. The reaction came with Peter, catechist, bishop and martyr. The record of Peter's life is scanty and its chronology uncertain. He was head of the catechetical school, probably in succession to Serapion; but it is uncertain whether he retained or resigned that office when he succeeded Theonas as bishop of Alexandria in 300. Eusebius has a word of high praise for his piety and his biblical knowledge, and describes him as "a splendid example of a teacher of the Christian faith[1]." But he says nothing of the literary work of Peter, perhaps because the library at Caesarea was not the place where anti-Origenistic writings would find a home[2]. More is known of his career as bishop. Three years after his consecration came the edict of Diocletian

---

[1] *H. E.* viii. 13. 7, θεῖόν τι χρῆμα διδασκάλων τῆς ἐν Χριστῷ εὐσεβείας. ix. 6. 2, θεῖον ἐπισκόπων χρῆμα βίου τε ἀρετῆς ἕνεκα καὶ τῆς τῶν ἱερῶν λόγων συνασκήσεως.

[2] Bardenhewer, ii. 204.

which struck at the Church through the clergy, and a
year later the fourth edict, which fell upon Christians
of all ranks; and when Diocletian abdicated, Maximin
instituted a fresh persecution which required all pro-
vincials to offer sacrifice to the pagan gods[1]. About
this time Peter fled, like Dionysius in 250, not to
secure his own safety but to save the church from the
loss of its guiding head. It is probable that he was
himself imprisoned for a time. It was in any case a
sorely tried episcopate[2] that closed with his martyrdom
on Nov. 25, 311. The problem of dealing with the
lapsed, those priests and people who had given way
before or under the strain of torture and incarceration,
was complicated and embittered by the agitation of
Meletius, who advocated a sterner policy than the
bishop thought wise under the varying circumstances
of the different cases; and the agitation broke out
into a schism of long and fierce continuance. We
are however concerned mainly here with Peter as a
theologian. Important questions of discipline and
organisation are involved in the so-called "canons" of
Peter which deal with this problem of the lapsed[3], and

[1] For the chronology of Peter's life, see Harnack, *Chron.* ii. 71,
72.

[2] Euseb. *H. E.* vii. 32. 31.

[3] These "canons" were once regarded as the work of a supposed
synod during the respite from persecution in 305; but they are now
recognised to be a fragment of an episcopal pronouncement of Peter's
own, perhaps an Easter pastoral (Harnack suggests a date, 306).
They are printed in Routh, *R. S.* iv. 23–45 (text), 52–76 (notes); also

in his letter warning the church of Alexandria against
Meletius[1]; but they contain practically nothing of
theological moment. The same is true of the Coptic
fragments of Peter edited by Schmidt and by Crum
respectively[2]. The " Acts " of the martyr-bishop are
similarly barren of doctrinal interest[3]. But amid their
strange blending of history and legend there is one touch
which at least bears witness to the prevalent impression
of Peter's theological attitude. In the farewell address
in which he foretells tribulation for the Church and
recalls its past troubles,—persecution in the episcopate
of Theonas, persecution and Sabellian heresy in the days
of Dionysius the Great,—he carries his retrospect back
to the time of " the blessed bishops Heraclas and
Demetrius." "What trials they endured from the mad-
ness of Origen, who gave rise to schisms in the Church
which stir up strife here unto this day[4]." It is this

in Migne, *Patr. Gr.* xviii. 467–508, with the scholia of the canonists
Balsamon and Zonaras.

[1] Migne, *op. cit.* pp. 509, 510; Routh, p. 51; Bardenhewer,
ii. 205.

[2] Schmidt, *Texte u. Unters.* xx. (N. F. v.), 4; Crum, *Journ. Theol.
Stud.*, April, 1903. A writer in *Analecta Bollandiana*, xx. (1901),
101–103, pronounced against the authenticity of Schmidt's fragment;
Harnack, *Chron.* ii. 74, 75, doubts them all as they stand; Crum
thinks certain passages " may indicate interpolated rather than
wholly apocryphal documents," *J. T. S.*, 1903, p. 387.

[3] On the question of their authenticity, see Harnack, *Chron.* ii.
74; Bardenhewer, ii. 210.

[4] Viteau, *Passions des Saints Ecaterine et Pierre d'Alexandrie*,
1897, p. 75.

antagonism to the peculiar doctrines of Origen which
constitutes the special theological interest of Peter's
work as a teacher and a writer. Unfortunately the
absence of indications of date in the surviving fragments
of his works precludes anything more than conjecture as
to the history of this antagonism. It may have been a
lifelong attitude, the outcome of early conviction, which
manifested itself from the very beginning of his work
as head of the catechetical school. On the other hand
it is possible that it was just his experience in the
school that led him to see and fear the dangers involved
in views which seemed to him more akin to Greek
speculation than to Christian piety; and these appre-
hensions may have been intensified by the pastoral
responsibilities which came with his promotion from the
teaching of Christian students to the care of all the
churches. In many ways Peter recalls and resembles
his predecessor Dionysius the Great. Dionysius indeed
seems to have felt the spell of Origen's influence more
strongly, or to have felt less keenly the divergence
between faith and enquiry; but both in Dionysius and
in Peter the pastor was predominant, though the
student was never lost.

Three fragments were cited by Cyril of Alexandria
at the council of Ephesus in 430 from a work of Peter's
entitled "On the Godhead" ($\pi\epsilon\rho\grave{\iota}$ $\Theta\epsilon\acute{o}\tau\eta\tau\sigma$)[1]. This

[1] Routh, *R. S.* iv. 46, 47 (text), 76, 77 (notes); Labbe's *Councils*,
iii. 508; Migne, *P. G.* xviii. 509–521.

title would seem at first sight to include the eternal as well as the temporal aspects of the doctrine of the Trinity; but the fragments of the work relate mainly to the Christology of the Incarnation. (1) The first passage deals with the *kenosis*. It is a mosaic of quotations from the New Testament. "Grace and truth indeed," says Peter, "came by Jesus Christ (John i. 17), whence also we have been saved by grace, according to the apostolic saying, and that not of ourselves, it is the gift of God, not of works, that a man may not boast (Eph. ii. 8, 9). By the will of God the Word being made flesh (John i. 1) and being found in fashion as a man (Phil. ii. 8) was not deprived of His divine nature. When He, being rich, became poor (2 Cor. viii. 9), it was not to forsake entirely His power or glory, but to take death upon Him for us sinners, the just for the unjust, that He might bring us to God, being put to death in the flesh but quickened in the spirit" (1 Pet. ii. 18). Practically we may take Peter of Alexandria as here asserting that what was laid aside in the Incarnation was not the possession but the exercise of divine attributes. There is insufficient material for a comparison of Peter with Origen in this matter of the *kenosis*. But roughly we may say that while Origen [1] regarded the limitation of the Word as a necessary sacrifice involved in the revelation of the

[1] e.g. *c. Celsum*, iv. 15.   See Bethune-Baker, *Intr. to Early Hist. Chr. Doctr.*, pp. 296, 297; Bigg, *Christian Platonists*, p. 262.

infinite God to finite man, Peter describes it here as a
deliberate part of the purpose of redemption. Origen
thinks of God revealing Himself in part to man ; Peter
thinks of God identifying Himself with man. Origen
lays more stress on the negative fact of the *kenosis*
itself, the veiling of the inherent glory; Peter on its
positive significance, the new glory of self-sacrificing love.

(2) The second fragment[1] deals with the Incarnation itself. Peter quotes the evangelist,—" The Word
became flesh, and dwelt among us " (John i. 14), and
proceeds, " from that time when the angel greeted the
Virgin, saying ' Hail, thou that art highly favoured, the
Lord is with thee ' " (Luke i. 28). Peter then explains
that " the Lord is with thee " means " God the Word is
with thee." " The angel thus signifies His being begotten in the womb and made flesh, as it is written, 'the
Holy Ghost shall come upon thee, and the power of the
most High shall overshadow thee, wherefore that holy
thing which is begotten shall be called Son of God ' "
(Luke i. 35).

(3) The third fragment is an emphatic statement of
the Virgin Birth. " God the Word, without the inter-
vention of a man[2], according to the will of God who is

[1] Printed in Syriac along with other Syriac fragments in Pitra (iv.
426) as a citation from the tractate *de Resurrectione* !

[2] παρὰ τὴν ἀνδρὸς ἀπουσίαν. Marius Mercator (Routh, iv. 47) trans.
" citra viri commercium "; Pitra trans. the Syriac version, " absque
viri concubitu." 'Απουσία = (1) absence, " in the absence of a man,"
(2) = ἀποσπερματισμός, " apart from the seed of a man."

able to accomplish all things, has been made flesh in
the womb of the Virgin, needing not the operation or
presence of a man; for the power of God overshadowing
the Virgin with the Holy Ghost that came upon her
wrought in her more effectually than a man."

Four Syriac fragments of this work on the Godhead
were printed by Pitra in his *Analecta Sacra* (vol. iv.
Syriac, pp. 187–194; Latin version, pp. 425, 426).
They are lettered by him A—D. A and C are the
first and third of the Greek fragments just described.
D is a single sentence which may have followed the
third Greek fragment, and is noteworthy as implying
the term *Theotokos*. "Therefore when Emmanuel was
born, He made the Virgin mother of God, having
taken flesh and birth of her in glorious wise." B is a
strenuous denial of the twofold personality of Christ.
It seems to have been a sequel to the second Greek
fragment, for it begins with the quotation of Luke i. 35
with which that fragment ends. It proceeds: "What
is born of flesh is flesh; but Mary gave birth in the
flesh to our Lord Jesus Christ, who is one and the same,
and not one and another,—God forbid. We say truly
that Jesus is Lord, believing especially that Jesus is
the Son of God, and that Jesus is Christ, just as it was
Jesus Himself who appeared to the apostles after His
ascension." The language of this fragment is opposed
to that Nestorian idea of the Son of God as being
merely in close association (συνάφεια) with the man

Jesus which drew from Cyril of Alexandria the sharper
assertion of two natures in complete union (ἕνωσις) in
one person. But we need not therefore suspect that
the extract is anti-Nestorian in date and purpose.
Cyril might have found such a passage in Peter's
treatise. Bardenhewer[1] however notes the extract
as suspicious on the ground that although the MS.
describes it as taken from the quotations made by
Cyril at the council of Ephesus, it is not to be found
in the extant text of the acts of that council.

Ephrem patriarch of Antioch, as we learn from
Photius[2], cited Peter along with Chrysostom and Basil
of Caesarea in proof of the statement that the doctrine
of the union of two natures (δύο φύσεων ἕνωσις) in
one person (μίαν ὑπόστασιν καὶ πρόσωπον ἕν) was
orthodox and apostolic. This appeal of Ephrem to the
teaching of Peter is justified by the fragment which
Leontius of Byzantium, in his treatise against Nes-
torians and Eutychians, quotes as from a work on the
earthly life of our Saviour (ἐκ τοῦ περὶ τῆς Σωτῆρος
ἡμῶν ἐπιδημίας)[3]. " He says to Judas, 'Betrayest thou
the Son of man with a kiss?' These words and the like,
and all the signs which he wrought and the mighty
works, show that He was God made man (Θεὸν εἶναι
ἐνανθρωπήσαντα). Both things indeed are shown,—

[1] *Altk. Litt.* ii. 208.
[2] *Cod.* 229, in Routh, *R. S.* iv. 50.
[3] Routh, *ib.*

that He was God by nature and has become man by nature" (ὅτι Θεὸς ἦν φύσει καὶ γέγονεν ἄνθρωπος φύσει). Peter evidently means that the miracles point to His divine nature, while the self-chosen title " Son of man " marks the reality of His human nature. The last sentence might well have been written deliberately to sum up the two truths endangered by Nestorianism and Eutychianism respectively. Nestorius combined two persons, the Son of God and the Son of man ; Eutyches combined two natures in one person, but by merging the human in the divine. The word γέγονεν on the contrary describes aptly the addition of the human nature to the divine nature of the one person, and also the permanence of that human nature in union with the divine. But we have no evidence to confirm or to disprove the traditional authorship of this fragment. Peter may have written such words in unconscious anticipation of later errors.

The five fragments of an Armenian version which have been printed by Pitra[1] are rejected by Bardenhewer[2] on the ground that they contain no certain indication of their origin. The first is practically identical with the doubtful Syriac fragment B. The second is shorter but similar in substance. Both insist on the reality of the human nature of the Word incarnate and upon the unity of His person. The third

[1] *Anal. S.* iv. 194 f. and 430.
[2] *Altk. Litt.* ii. 210.

lllll

breaks new ground. It is an anathema against those who "venture to say that the union (of the two natures) was defiled by the body (corpore corruptam fuisse unionem) or to divide God from the body," i.e. to separate the divine nature from the human. The first half of this sentence is apparently a fusion of two such statements as (a) that the Godhead was defiled by the body, and (b) that the union of the Godhead with the body was a defilement. Its purport seems to be a protest against the half-gnostic depreciation of the human nature of the Word incarnate. It was some such depreciation as this which was seen or suspected in much of Origen's teaching with reference to the human nature of our Lord, e.g. in his hesitation to admit the permanence of that human nature after the Ascension[1].

The fourth fragment speaks the language of sheer monophysitism. "God and the body together are but one nature and one person, who came by His own will and by the dispensation of the Spirit. This one person is to be adored as God indivisible in this indivisible unity." This indivisible unity is apparently not the unity of the one Godhead of the undivided Trinity, but the unity of the one person of Christ and that divine. But Pitra, the editor of the fragment, rightly deprecates the language being pressed word for word. Its context is unknown, and its supposed date is prior

[1] e.g. *Hom. in Jerem.* xv., *in Luc.* xxix. ; Redepenning, ii. 313 f.

to the outbreak of the controversy over the two natures.
Cyril of Alexandria could not merely write μίαν φύσιν
τοῦ Λόγου σεσαρκωμένην, but could claim for this
expression or for its substance the authority of "the
fathers[1]," without any idea that the expression would
lay him open to the risk of seeming in his turn to
authorise heresy.

The fifth fragment however is even more precise
and emphatic in the direction of monophysitism.
"Those who after the indivisible union speak of two
natures, two appearances, two Sons, one owing His origin
to the Father, the other to His mother Mary, are guilty
of folly. They dishonour the Father by recognising
two Sons, one natural, the other adventitious. Thus
they introduce a quaternity, and in their discourses
practically deny the Holy Trinity. A new God is
adored who has His origin from Mary. Further, if
these things be so, the whole Christian world has gone
wrong in adoring a man who has been crucified and in
eating his body and blood." This is a reasoned indict-
ment of the logical results of the Nestorianism which
saw in the Incarnation merely the association of two
persons. Such a passage is incredible at any other
period than that in which Nestorianism stood revealed
in its development and its bearings. The language is
too pointed for a pre-Nestorian, still more for a pre-

---

[1] See the discussion of this phrase in Ottley's *Doctrine of the
Incarnation*, ii. 93 f.

Nicene writer. The first two of these Armenian
fragments may perhaps be genuine. But these last
three fragments can scarcely be defended. The last
confirms the doubts raised by the others. Bardenhewer
would have been nearer the mark if he had rejected
them all on the ground that they did contain certain
indications of their origin, and that origin plainly anti-
Nestorian and therefore post-Nestorian.

The Christology of the apparently genuine fragments
of these two works of Peter "On the Godhead" and
"On the coming of the Saviour"—if indeed they are
two and not one—presents practically no point of direct
and overt divergence from Origen. Harnack indeed
says (*Hist. of Dogma*, E. Tr. iii. 99) that Peter "maintains
against Origen the complete humanity of the Redeemer,
the creation of our souls with our bodies, and the
historical character of the events narrated in Gen. iii.
&c." The last two assertions are true, as we shall see,
but the first is at least an over-statement. Origen can
scarcely be said to have denied the complete humanity
of our Lord. There were certainly three points on
which his teaching on this subject was peculiar. (1) His
idea of the human soul of Christ is open to the objection
that on his own theory of souls it was not a soul at all[1].
It was removed from absolute likeness to human souls
by its prenatal union with the Word. It was brought
by the Word to the body of His incarnation rather than

[1] Redepenning, ii. 387 ; Bigg, *op. cit.* p. 190, n. 1.

taken with the body by the Word. (2) He regarded
the manhood of the ascended Christ as in some way
merged and absorbed in His Deity. (3) There was a
touch of Docetism in his idea of the varying appearances
of our Lord to different persons during His earthly
life[1]. Now as far as Origen's view of our Lord's soul
is bound up with his theory of the nature of a human
soul, it is certainly controverted by Peter's teaching on
that subject, as we shall see. But with regard to the
two other peculiarities of Origen, though they are
certainly incompatible with the teaching of Peter,
yet there is nothing in the Christological fragments of
Peter which can be described as directed against the
teaching of Origen. Harnack himself qualifies his own
language when he says that Peter's " own expositions
on the other hand show that he only deprived Origen's
doctrines of their extreme conclusions, while otherwise
he maintained them in so far as they did not come
into direct conflict with the rule of faith." Perhaps it
would be true to say that Origen could have assented
to all that Peter says in these Christological fragments,
but that Origen had said many things to which Peter
could not have assented.

On other questions, however, the divergence is a
matter of unmistakable evidence or of not unwarrantable
inference. The leniency of letter and spirit alike which
marks the " canons " of Peter with reference to the

[1] *c. Cels.* iv. 16.

treatment of the lapsed is akin to the example and
policy of Dionysius the Great[1]. Origen on the other
hand had been the strictest of the strict in his earlier
views of discipline, though in later days his stern
principles were somewhat tempered by a hopeful
recognition of wider possibilities of forgiveness[2]. The
rigidity so natural in the enthusiast and the scholar
stands in clear contrast to the attitude of the two
bishops. Prompted by disposition or taught by circum-
stance, they made wise provision for the future of those
weaker brethren who had tried, though they had failed,
to stand firm under trial; and at the same time they
made a fearless protest against the fanaticism of
martyrdom in those stronger brethren whose gratuitous
provocation of the authorities often ended in their own
lapse as well as in a fiercer persecution of the faithful
at large. It would however be pure supposition to read
in Peter's canons any reference to Origen's attitude on
this great question. They were directed against a
contemporary danger. Neither is it necessary or
justifiable to regard them as a deliberate exculpation
of his own example of flight[3].

[1] See Feltoe, *Dionysius*, p. 5.

[2] Bigg, *op. cit.* pp. 217, 218. Tixeront, *Théologie Ante-Nicéenne*,
pp. 300, 301, suggests that Origen's more lenient passages may have
owed their leniency to the revising hand of his Latin translator in the
fourth century.

[3] Schmidt so regards them, *Fragm. e. Schrift. d. Märtyrer-Bischofs
Petrus v. Alexandrien*, in *Texte u. Unters.* xx. (N.F. v.), 4, pp. 18-20.
Bardenhewer (ii. 306, n. 1) rejects the idea.

The three notes of Origenistic teaching against
which Peter does exhibit an undoubted reaction are
(1) the allegorical interpretation of Holy Scripture,
(2) the belief in the preexistence of souls, (3) the
denial of the material identity of the resurrection body
with the earthly body. (1) Origen for example had
explained the coats of skins with which God clothed
Adam and Eve as representing bodies in which the
souls that had sinned were clothed when they were
cast out of the paradise of their earlier existence into
the punishment of an earthly life, and again as
symbolising the liability of sinful man to death[1].
Procopius in his commentary on Genesis cites Dionysius
and Peter amongst others as repudiating the allegorical
interpretation of these coats of skins and other details
of the story of Paradise[2]. Some doubt has been cast
upon the accuracy of this statement with regard to
Dionysius, whose attitude in matters of scriptural
interpretation is hard to define[3]. He was a fearless
yet reverent critic of the Apocalypse; and he was not
afraid of allegorism in principle, though he was careful
to avoid its eccentricities in practice. On the whole
we are not in a position to deny the statement of
Procopius with regard to Dionysius, and we have no
need to doubt his accuracy with regard to Peter.

---

[1] *Comm. in Genes.* iii. 21 ; *c. Cels.* iv. 40.

[2] Routh, *R. S.* iv. 50, 78.

[3] Feltoe, *Dionysius*, pp. xxvii, xxviii, 229.

(2) Origen had not merely taught the bare pre-existence of the soul. He had seen in this preexistence a solution of the moral and physical inequalities of this life, though he had not fully faced the fact that this solution merely pushed the problem further back into the earlier existence which he postulated. Here was a graver issue even than the question of the interpretation of Scripture. Peter turned from theology to psychology. He followed up his great work on the Godhead by a series of sermons or treatises in contradiction of this dangerous belief that the soul had not merely existed before the body, but had been sent into the body in consequence of its sin in that previous stage of its existence. The opening words of the larger fragment of the first of these discourses seem to imply that Peter was sensible of a connexion of some sort between Christology and anthropology. "Having set forth first," he writes, "the things that concern the Godhead and humanity of the second man from heaven, as the blessed apostle calls Him (1 Cor. xv. 47), we thought it needful to set forth also the things that concern the first man, who has been made of the earth earthy, in order to show that he was made one and the same at the same moment[1]." We are not meant perhaps to press the parallel, any more than we can press the parallel of the *Quicunque vult*,—"for as the reasonable soul and flesh is one man, so God and man is one

[1] Routh, *R. S.* iv. 48, 49.

Christ." It might be argued on the contrary that the
preexistence of the divine nature of the Son before its
union with human nature in the Incarnation was
suggestive of the preexistence of the soul before its
union with a body in man. It is not Peter's intention
to elaborate a comparison between the two natures in
Christ and the two elements, soul and body, in man's
nature. His meaning seems rather to be this, that the
consideration of the human nature in union with the
divine leads appropriately to the consideration of human
nature in itself.

It is true, Peter admits, that man is sometimes
described in Scripture as consisting of the outward and
the inward man. But this is simply an analysis of man
as he is. When the Saviour says, " He that made the
inside made the outside also[1] " (Lk. xi. 40), He is
referring to one single creative act which took place
when God said, " Let us make man after our image
and likeness " (Gen. i. 26). It is clear from this, Peter
says, that man has not come into being by a combination, as though the one part of him were preexistent
and had come from elsewhere to join the other part.
If there were a combination of this sort, why should
that which had on this hypothesis already been created

---

[1] κατὰ τὸν Σωτήριον λόγον, Ὁ ποιήσας τὰ ἔσωθεν καὶ τὰ ἔξωθεν ἐποί-
ησεν. The received text of Lk. xi. 40 stands thus : οὐχ ὁ ποιήσας τὸ
ἔξωθεν καὶ τὸ ἔσωθεν ἐποίησε ; It is quoted thus by Cyril, Marcion
(Tertullian), and Augustine. But CD and some cursives give τὸ ἔσωθεν
καὶ τὸ ἔξωθεν, and Cyprian twice quotes this reading.

be recorded as part of the new creation[1]? Peter says, "It is clear from this," i.e. from the fiat of creation, "Let us make man, &c." His argument seems to run thus. The words of Scripture prove that the part of man's being which constitutes his likeness to God was included in the fiat of creation, i.e. was at that moment non-existent. But it is the soul which constitutes that likeness. Therefore the soul cannot have been pre-existent. A further argument is adduced from the case of other living things. If the rest of the animals brought forth by the earth were endowed with life then and there by God's command, so too the soil taken from the earth to form man must have received its living power then and there by the will and operation of God. Peter evidently means that if there is no suggestion of preexistence in the case of animal life, there can be no ground for supposing preexistence in the case of human life.

In the one Syriac fragment which is attributed expressly to this work on the soul (Pitra, *Anal. S.* iv. 193–4 Syriac, 429 Latin version), Peter quotes Matt. x. 28, the Lord's warning to fear Him who can destroy both body and soul in hell. The conclusion which he draws thence is that the body slain by men rises again in reunion with the soul, so that body and soul may receive together the joint reward of their deeds. Peter is asserting the joint responsibility of both elements of

[1] $\tau i \nu o s$ $\ddot{\epsilon} \nu \epsilon \kappa \epsilon \nu$ $\kappa a \dot{\iota}$ $\tau \dot{o}$ $\pi \epsilon \pi o \iota \eta \mu \dot{\epsilon} \nu o \nu$ $\dot{a} \nu \epsilon \gamma \rho \dot{a} \phi \eta$;

man's being for the sins of the whole man, as against
the Origenists who regarded the body itself as a
retribution for the sin of the preexistent soul.

The second Greek fragment is but a single sentence
summing up the position. "It is not possible for souls
to sin in heaven before (their union with) bodies, since
they have not even existed before bodies. This doctrine
belongs to Greek philosophy, which is foreign and alien
to them that desire to live a godly life in Christ."
This is a strangely uncompromising judgment for a
scholar-bishop of Alexandria to pass upon Greek
thought. It is therefore a happy discovery to find it
balanced by the last of Pitra's Syriac fragments, which,
though unassigned, is apparently a survival of this work
on the soul. "It is the proper task of Christianity to
give to each age in succession a knowledge free from
error, and to lead to happiness of life those who are
being perfected by that knowledge." Peter was no foe
to learning as such. He only insisted on its being
kept sound in character and true to its spiritual end.
Harnack aptly remarks: "this word shows that Peter,
opponent of Origen as he was, yet stood within the
circle of his ideas[1]."

(3) Peter's view of the manner of the resurrection
can be gathered with sufficient clearness from the
copious fragments which Pitra has collected of the
Syriac version of an important treatise on this very

[1] *Altchr. Litt.* i. 447.

subject. So reconstructed, his view stands in direct
opposition to that of Origen[1]. Origen had taught that
the resurrection body would be a new growth from the
germinative principle which was all that would survive
of the old body, the material elements of that body
having been scattered and absorbed into other substances
and organisms. He insisted indeed on the necessity of
the identity of the future with the present body, if there
was to be any real or just reward or retribution for the
share of the present body in the good or evil works of
the soul. But he regarded this identity as secured by
the recognition of a *ratio* or principle of individual life
which would survive the dissolution of the old body, and
would reappear as the formative essence of the new, just
as it had survived the gradual change of every particle
of matter year by year in the old body. It is difficult
to see where Origen believed this germ to reside or
whether he had any definite idea of its nature. It is
no less difficult to reconcile this whole idea of the
resurrection with his view of the body as a retribution
for the sin of the preexistent soul, or again with his
view of martyrdom as lifting the soul at once to the
highest level of existence, and that a purely spiritual
existence. But there is no doubt that to Origen
himself this theory of the resurrection was the simple
working out of the Pauline analogy of the identity of

[1] Redepenning, ii. 118–127 ; Bigg, *op. cit.* pp. 192, n. 1, 198, n. 1,
225–226.

seed and plant. Peter asserts on the contrary that such a growth as Origen supposes would be not a change but an exchange. It involved nothing of the miraculous. It was not strictly speaking a resurrection at all. " What resurrection in the proper sense of the word can that be which does not raise up what has fallen or revive what has perished or renew what has worn away ?" The resurrection meant to Peter the rising again of the old body transfigured by a new glory.

The possibility of such a resurrection, he argues, is simply a question of the power of the Creator. He appeals to the names given to the body. It is called a building, as being fashioned of earthly material; it is called a work, as being the product of a personal agent. That same creative power which gave life to man's mortal frame at the beginning can raise him from the dead. Peter is forgetful or regardless of the scorn which Origen had poured upon this appeal to the omnipotence of the Creator. Origen styled this argument the refuge of the unreasoning[1]. Peter insists that the believer is confirmed in his faith on this point by the wonderful works of God from the beginning of the world. The incredulous he confronts with the challenge which S. Paul threw down to the unbeliever of his day to show ground for his unbelief (Acts xxvi. 8). At the same time Peter points to the language of

[1] c. Cels. v. 23, ἀποπωτάτη ἀναχώρησις.

Scripture as not satisfied by anything less than a rising again of the body.

The scriptural proof of this identity of the old and the new body is drawn from the relation between Christ and His people. At the beginning there is the resemblance of creation (Gen. i. 26),—man made in the image and after the likeness of God. In the end there shall be the resemblance of consummation,—"when He shall appear, we shall be like Him, for we shall see Him as He is" (1 John iii. 2). Between these two stages of human destiny lies the resurrection of the Christ who is the "first-begotten from the dead" and the "first-fruits of them that slept." His resurrection leads the way and marks the manner. His risen body was the body which was buried, as indeed He proved to His disciples (Luke xxiv. 39, John xx. 27). So will ours be also.

Peter is aware that the incredulous are perplexed by the plain assertion of S. Paul that "flesh and blood cannot inherit the kingdom of heaven" (1 Cor. xv. 50). But, he argues, S. Paul says "cannot inherit," not "cannot rise again." Flesh and blood as they are spell corruption, the physical corruption of disease and death, the moral corruption of sin. It is this sad sequence of sin and death that destroys the possibility of immortality for man as he is now[1]. Peter then

[1] We know from Irenaeus (v. 9. 1) that S. Paul's words (1 Cor. xv. 50) were used by heretics of every type as an argument against the

quotes 1 Cor. iii. 7 as illustrating the connexion
between moral and physical corruption,—"if any man
defile the temple of God, him shall God destroy." He
insists that by flesh and blood the apostle means human
nature as a whole, just as elsewhere *caro* is used in the
sense of *homo totus*. The apostle is asserting the
necessity of a change before that glorious destiny can
be realised; he is not denying the possibility of such a
change as would be compatible with a real identity.

This change we shall all undergo (1 Cor. xv. 51),
for we shall "all rise again and bring again our own
bodies according to our deeds, good or evil" (2 Cor. v. 10),
and therefore we all need this change. Peter's idea
of this change is of course vague and undefinable.
"Crowned with glory and honour we shall come forth
so firm and strong that the body will be able to bear
the splendour of the heavenly air, since each one will
be brought to immortality and incorruption." Neither
does he throw any light upon the difference between
the dead who will rise incorruptible and the living who
will simply be "changed." In fact he seems to say
that the change will be the same for both. But it is
noteworthy that his language permits, if it does not

Church's doctrine. Irenaeus replies that S. Paul is speaking "of the
flesh considered apart from the Spirit, i.e. human nature unsanctified
and unrenewed" (Swete, *Apostles' Creed*, p. 93). Tertullian's answer
is an even closer parallel to Peter's; S. Paul, he protests, does not
say that the flesh shall not rise, but that it must undergo a change
before it can enter the kingdom (*de resurr. carnis*, c. 50).

require, the reversal of S. Paul's distinction between himself and his readers on the one hand and those on the other hand who have or shall have departed this life. Peter speaks of himself and his readers as "receiving again our bodies once laid in the tomb," while "those who shall remain alive shall retain their own bodies." The "day of the Lord," so near to the believer of two hundred years ago, has already receded far into the distant future.

The manner of the change is illustrated from the Transfiguration and Resurrection of the Lord. At the Transfiguration He was "changed," but took no other body in place of His own, retaining the same human body in which He had climbed the mount with His disciples. After the Resurrection again He was "changed." The disciples thought that they saw a spirit, and failed to recognise their Lord. So too our bodies will be changed when they put on the body which is not animal but spiritual (1 Cor. xv. 44). Peter stays a moment here to guard against a mis-interpretation of this key-word "change." "It is well known that the blessed Paul is after the customary manner of speech using the word *change* in the simple sense of *variation*." Peter adds that of course there is another use of the word in the sense of *exchange* which occurs in figurative speech and is approved in Holy Scripture, especially in the Law, e.g. Exod. xiii. 13,

xxxiv. 20. His one anxiety is to safeguard the idea of identity in the midst of change.

Finally this change is attributed to the operation of the Holy Spirit. As in the creation, as in the awakening of the dry bones in the valley, so in the resurrection of the dead. "'I will pour my Spirit upon you,' so runs the prophecy, to teach us that it is by the glory of the Holy Spirit that the bodies of the just are to be enlightened with immortality, with incorruption, with glory and brightest splendour. It is plain that the resurrection consists not in a change of nature but in a garment won for us by grace, whereby when death and corruption are put to flight there begins an eternal abiding, with a glorious participation of the nature of God."

Jerome says that Origen complained of two errors in the Church of his day,—the error of the heretic who denied any resurrection at all, and the error of the orthodox who took the identity of the risen body to mean nothing less than the reproduction of every member in its old matter, form and function[1]. Peter can scarcely be accused of a crude conception of this kind. He insists upon the necessity of a change in the conditions of the body with an emphasis which is not diminished by the vagueness of the little that he says about the character and extent of this change.

[1] *Ep.* 38 *ad Pammach.*

On the other hand it is impossible to mistake the sharpness of the separation between his view and that of Origen. Peter postulates the recovery of the lost matter; Origen denies both the necessity and the possibility of such a recovery. Both Origen and Peter indeed claim to be in line with the teaching of S. Paul, and both insist upon the continuity of the body as a necessary element of a true resurrection. But Origen believed this continuity to be secured by the permanence of a principle or germ of life, while Peter thought that its only security lay in the revival of the constituent elements, even though they were revived only to undergo a transfiguration. Origen is easier to reconcile with modern scientific thought; but Peter's view is nearer to the only idea that we can form of the transition of the living bodies of those who shall survive until the coming of the Lord.

It is interesting to note the line of the contemporary attack upon Origen's doctrine of the resurrection which came from the pen of Methodius, bishop of Olympus in Lycia, who died the death of a martyr about the time of Peter's own martyrdom[1]. It has been supposed that Methodius was the opponent whom Pamphilus had in mind in framing his famous defence of Origen. His was certainly the most comprehensive and decided

---

[1] For Methodius and his writings, see Bardenhewer, ii. 291 f., especially 299, 300; for his teaching, Harnack, *Hist. of Dogma*, E. Tr. iii. 104–112, especially 105, 106.

opposition, though Peter's opposition was scarcely less
important both from its own force and from the prestige
of his authority as bishop of Alexandria. The fragments
of Peter's work deal mainly with the identity of the
risen body in itself. Methodius in his dialogue on the
resurrection treats this identity as part of the whole
destiny of man. He grapples with Origen's idea of
human life as a whole. For Methodius the whole man
is by creation immortal in body and soul. The separation of body and soul is the result of sin marring the
image of God in man. Death is the casting of God's
marred work into the crucible again; the resurrection
is the recasting of the work, to be clothed anew with
its primal glory. Something of this idea is to be
seen in Peter also. In his insistence upon the moral
necessity of the identity of the risen body as well as
of the soul, if the whole man is to receive the due
reward of his deeds, he seems to be challenging the
Origenistic view which practically regarded the soul as
the man and the body as the penal accident of the
soul's earthly existence. Both Methodius and Peter
remind us that the resurrection is part of the re-
demptive work of God, the fulfilment after all of the
original purpose of man's creation. It is a stage in
the evolution of the whole man. If Origen is more
philosophical in his forecast of the way in which the
body shall rise, Peter and Methodius are more philosophical in setting the resurrection in its true relation

to the creation of man. Origen himself, with a happy
inconsistency, drops the idea of the body as the penalty
of the sin of the soul when he turns to speculate upon
the destiny of human nature. Yet on the question of
the manner of the resurrection Origen left a mark
upon Greek theology which not all the subsequent
criticism of the weak or dangerous points of his theory
could efface. When the revision of the Eastern creeds
in the fourth century replaced " the resurrection of the
flesh" by "the resurrection of the dead," it was probably
the influence of Origen that led to the supersession of
a phrase which had once served the Church well " as a
protest against a false spirituality " but had come to be
" pressed to the length of a crude materialism[1]." The
phrase " the resurrection of the body " was not without
ambiguity or suspicion. At an early stage in the controversy Pamphilus quotes the opponents of Origen
as asserting that he admitted indeed the resurrection
of the body but denied the resurrection of the flesh[2];
and at a later stage Jerome tells us that the orthodox
thought that the word *body* in that phrase meant *flesh*,
but the heretic understood it to mean *spirit*[3]. The
Eastern creeds fell back upon the words " the resurrection of the dead," which left the manner of the
resurrection an open question. The West still kept

[1] Swete, *Apostles' Creed*, pp. 94–98.
[2] Routh, *R. S.* iv. 378.
[3] *Ep.* 41 *ad Pamm. et Oceanum.*

"the resurrection of the flesh." The formularies of the English Church, here as in so many places consciously or unconsciously gathering together the witness of all the sundered parts of Christendom, retain not only "the resurrection of the dead," which marks the universality of that great event, but also "the resurrection of the body," which marks "the restoration of the individual life," and "the resurrection of the flesh," which marks "the continuity of the restored life with that which has gone before[1]." The two distinct elements of the truth for which Origen and Peter respectively stood are thus blended with the wider language which was finally adopted by their Church as the wisest authoritative statement of the mystery. The elements of error on either side fell off or were thrown away, to return or revive indeed wherever the same temper of bold speculation or of anxious conservatism is found; but the key-words upon which each disputant in turn laid stress all stand in our formularies to-day as symbols of integral parts of that truth which survives alike denial and exaggeration.

[1] Swete, *op. cit.* p. 98.

GENERAL INDEX.

"standard" of creation, 18–20 ; His titles, 20–25 ; His ἐπίνοιαι, 24; His unity, 26, 27; His immutability, 27

Soul of Christ, 69, 70

Spirit, the Holy, 4, 5, 52 ; limitation of His action, 30 f. ; His work in the resurrection, 82

Stephanus Gobar, 2

Subordinationism, 23, 35

Syriac fragments of Peter Alex., 64, 65, 75, 76

Theodore of the Studium, 55

Theodorus of Alexandria, 45

Theognostus, ix, 1–43

Theonas, 1 n., 44, 45, 46 n., 58, 60

Theotokos, 47, 56, 64

Transfiguration of Christ, 81

Trinity, the Holy, 9, 11, 68 ; distinctions of sphere or function, 30 f.

Trinity, neo-platonist, 21 n.

Unity of the Son, 26, 27, 67

Virgin Birth, 57, 63

Wisdom, 21, 22

Word, the, 21, 22

INDEX OF GREEK WORDS.

For EU product safety concerns, contact us at Calle de José Abascal, 56–1°,
28003 Madrid, Spain or eugpsr@cambridge.org.

www.ingramcontent.com/pod-product-compliance
Ingram Content Group UK Ltd.
Pitfield, Milton Keynes, MK11 3LW, UK
UKHW020312140625
459647UK00018B/1836